Angela Leighton was born in Wakefield,
educated in Edinburgh and Oxford, and
has taught at the universities of Hull
and Cambridge. She is Research Fellow
in poetry at Trinity College, Cambridge
and has published many works of literary
criticism, poetry and short stories. Her
three previous collections of poetry are
A Cold Spell (2000), *Sea Level* (2007), and
The Messages (2012).

First published in Great Britain in 2016
by Carcanet Press Limited, Alliance House,
30 Cross Street, Manchester, M2 7AQ
www.carcanet.co.uk

Typeset by LA in Arnhem Pro & Averta. A CIP
catalogue record for this book is available from
the British Library, ISBN 9781847772251.

The publisher acknowledges financial assistance
from Arts Council England.

Angela
Leighton
Spills

CARCANET

Contents

Canticles for a Passion

Translations from Leonardo Sciascia

Spill

—*splinter or rod*

—*strip for lighting a pipe or fire*

—*wooden spindle or spool*

—*rod of wood, bone or plastic in a
  game of spillikins*

—*pin for stopping a cask*

—*channel for carrying water*

—*overflow or puddle of liquid*

—*small gift of money*

'Can these bones live?'

– Ezekiel

✳

'*Come andò che maestro Ciliegia, falegname, trovò un pezzo di legno, che piangeva e rideva come un bambino.*'

[How it came about that Master Cherry, carpenter, found a piece of wood, which wept and laughed like a child.]

– Carlo Collodi, *Pinocchio*

✳

'The whole fabric that he had been building, like a game of spillikins in which one frail little bone is hooked on top of another, was dashed to the ground.'

– Virginia Woolf, *Night and Day*

✳

'Roped in at the end by the one
Death with its many sticks.'

– Sylvia Plath, 'Totem'

for Harriet, fellow traveller

Bog Asphodel

Once, by Elgol,
under ikat sunsets, driving affluent rain,
my two-ply tongue,
tongue-tied for weeks, word-stuck in kind, recognised:
bog asphodel.

To a cold conditioning ground, unpastured space,
its Delphic heavenly
ring brought sandalled toes, Elysian meadows,
Athens, Rome—
gilding the peat bog, winning a pot of gold.

Asphodel—
long echo. Here on the bare, bone-breaking heath
my tongue's bell,
bi-lingual, local, levies a name from elsewhere,
and finds its place.

*Life
from
Sixteen
Angles*

Preface

Angles, not angels—though angels lurk among the letters somewhere, subject to some calligraphic reordering, slips of the tongue, trips or typos. But *angles* are different. They might be acute or obtuse, needlingly sharp or widely blunt. There's no trusting words, though the journey we take, reading or writing, can trust to nothing else. There's no other vehicle on the seas of memory upon which we set out whenever we put pen to paper, fingers to keys, or just eye to print.

This particular journey is a glancing one, angled and refracted like the light in the atmosphere. And although it might be described as a journey, an old story that goes from childhood to adulthood, early to later years, it also goes back and forth, like the various actual journeys of my life—its sense of progression stalled by returns of memory, hauntings from other places, etymological double-takes. The very language, of course, is full of its own memories: foreign derivations at work in the English, quotations and allusions jostling for attention, older senses layering beneath the new. The language was never simply indigenous, never just our own. It was always a migrant from other times, other places.

This, then, is a story that falls out, as most stories do, from a mix of life's unprospected accidents and later patterns of retrospection. Although its narratives are based on fact and its characters known to me, the shape they take depends on a certain design, a discovery of connections and motifs which only came clear in the writing, as loose spills might settle into a picture. Chapters may be as short as snapshots or as long as stories, angled as documentary memoir or indirect short fiction. Their point is not so much to delineate characters, least of all myself, as to open an ear to the poem or the music to which they give rise, or from which they spring. The forms of memoir, story, prose poem and poem are always permeable, always sliding across thin walls into one another—and this is no exception. Like that first fallout of who we are, thrown together from an ancient random mix of inherited genes, the structure might recall a game of spillikins. These splinters or fragments, spills or spells, are a reminder that what we remember, even of ourselves, is only a haphazard thing of bits and pieces—a thing which language itself, whether prosaic, poetic or even translated, might try to join together again.

1—Pa Bu

Musica, musica, che vuoi da me?
Che corpo sta formandosi
lungo la tua catena di molecole?
Che traccia sto seguendo mentre vado
dietro le note come dietro briciole
lasciate da qualcuno per ritornare a casa?
A quale casa mi fai ritornare?

– Valerio Magrelli

[Music, music, what do you want from me?
What kind of body is forming
along your molecular chain?
What trace am I following as I go
after the notes, as if after crumbs
left by someone to show the way home?
To which home would you have me return?]

It was a small room, anaglypta wallpaper swirling in fronds, a
dark upright piano against one wall, a barrel-shaped biscuit tin
on the hearth and, on the mantelpiece, three grey monkeys sitting
side by side, their too human hands covering eyes, ears or mouth.
Were they playing some kind of blind man's bluff, sharing a joke,
or keeping a secret? She eyed them distrustfully.

On the floor where she crawled, empty cotton-reels lay scattered in
all directions. They were roly-poly, warm-wooden to touch, chew-
able, even flavoursome in a queer way. They could be marched in
rows, dull, identical and featureless, or built into rickety columns for
knocking. With a swipe of her arm, she could send those chattery
woodenheads knocking together to the edge of the carpet. *Bobbins,*
Nanny repeated, holding one out, uncertain what else to say to this
sullen, dark-eyed child who merely stared at her, wonderingly.

Those bobbins were the only toy in the house—the saved residue
of years of labour, when each week she took in the neighbours'
mending, and spent her days patching, paring, repairing at the
heavy sewing machine upstairs. It was black and gold, a growling,
stomping creature called a Singer, that made the floor shake and
the ceiling lamps sway. Up and down, up and down, her feet would
work the ponderous iron treadle, while yards of cloth slipped under
the furious piston of the needle. It was labour which depended on
that pedestrian rhythm: slow and halting for the awkward collars
and plackets, fast and easy as she ran the long hems between the

pressure-foot and the throat-plate. Then, her fingers would dance round the eye of the needle, keeping the cloth taut and moving as the machine jabbed its thread into the weave. They were light and limber, those fingers, dancing for their lives, while her feet kept up their relentless tread, beating out time like some hard taskmaster. The heartbeat of that bass line thudded through the small house, audible everywhere: in the kitchen below, in the three-yard square of garden with its outdoor lavatory, and through the walls to the long-suffering neighbours.

Yet hers were also musician's fingers. They knew their way round the piano's blocks of sound, the tonic or plagal cadences of its hymns, the quick harmonic changes of its folksongs. Nanny played by ear, her listening fingers picking out the shapes of tunes in her head and touching them instantly into life. She played *Abide With Me*, *Old King Cole*, the *Hokey Cokey*. The piano, which made nothing out of nothing except songs to fill your ears, was like a mirror image of the other Singer upstairs, which clunked and whirred, clattered and thumped, churning out frocks, jackets, aprons—things made to measure, useful and paid for. One of the things it helped to pay for was the expensive manuscript paper constantly clamoured for by her difficult younger son. At first she insisted he drew the staves himself, ruling them on white sheets of paper. When, however, she discovered he was slipping buttons into the collection plate at church, and pocketing the coins she gave him in order to buy manuscript paper from the music shop, she relented. This, perhaps, was more than a childhood whim. One day he would indeed pay the church back for those filched offerings—pay over the odds in the quantity of church music he would agree to write for it. Perhaps he paid his mother back, too, many years later, in this, the only currency he knew.

She taught him to play the piano herself, but very quickly he surpassed everything she knew. At six, he was picking out her tunes, embellishing them, improvising, and as soon as he became a choirboy at the cathedral, aged eight, he was writing the notes down, making tiny whiskery dots on those yellowish sheets bought at such cost. Sitting at the piano, hour after hour, year after year, in that tiny terraced two-up two-down, parents and older brother suffering the noise, he turned out jazzy, syncopated rhythms, trialled dissonances and false relations, returned to lyrical sweeps of melody, against the routine wheels of the Singer upstairs—his fingers against hers, or else, more truly, his fingers within hers, as she battled on the other unwieldy instrument to help pay for the music he needed to make.

Perhaps it was only when she died, many years later, helpless and pitiful in the local asylum, that he realised what he owed her. Then,

Life from Sixteen Angles

through months of anguished remembrance, he returned the gift, writing the symphony that he dedicated to her—a dark, macabre, witty piece, that might at moments of jazzy playfulness be remembering the sound of her fingers on the piano in that tiny, cluttered front room in Wakefield.

✕

'Bobbin?' she asked again, holding one out as if offering the novelty of a word amidst a superfluity of dull things. It sounded funny in the child's ears, and she frowned, refusing to repeat the senseless noise. Instead, she let out a whimper, and dashed one of them to the edge of the room where, on hitting the wall, it made a satisfying wooden click. 'Naughty naughty', the voice reproved, incomprehensible except for the tone. But its tone was enough to break the child's restraint—the thing that had kept her miserably focussed on those little wooden drums that rolled wilfully here and there, chit-chatting together in their own language. Suddenly, she let out a wail of misery. It came out loud as could be, while tears filled her eyes. 'Pa bu', she bawled, choking on her own words, then even louder and clearer, dragging on each sound: 'Pa bu, pa bu'. In it was all the bewilderment and terror of this, her first experience of being left alone, without mamma, in her grandmother's house. Everything was foreign in it: the carpet, the cold brown tiles of the hearth, and above all the voices—hushed, reticent voices that spoke strange words in disapproving tones. Those bobbins, she knew somewhere in her child's mind, were a decoy, a distraction from the conspiracy of betrayal that had left her there. She didn't want bobbins, those hard, dry things; she wanted pa bu. And the more she wailed, the more she wanted it, in a world where everything seemed secretive, misunderstood, where cries made no difference.

So she wept, hiccuped and sobbed with the abandon of the lost. Nanny, in a fluster, brought a biscuit, a glass of milk; she held out the horrible row of monkeys; in desperation, she pulled a funny face and waggled her hands like ears. Ever more enraged at this madness of the world around her, at everything, it seemed, turned deaf and stupid, the child stared for a moment, then continued to bawl hopelessly, miserably: 'Pa bu'.

Eventually, exhausted, she fell asleep, rocked on Nanny's lap while she sang, very softly: 'Golden slumbers kiss your eyes; Smiles await you when you rise.' Much later, when she awoke, it was at the sound of a door closing, voices coming clearer, and then a familiar voice apologising, explaining: '*Scusa, mi dispiace.* So sorry. I should have explained. What she likes is pa bu – *pane e burro.* It's bread and butter.'

2—Swings and Roundabouts

The city was huge and dark. It towered above her as they walked down the street, her father clutching her hand tight, as if uncertain of his hold. Usually she went with Mamma, but he'd promised to take her to the playground one day when he wasn't working. They trudged together along the stony streets, both of them newcomers to this northern city, both of them still somehow feeling their way. Outings with her father were rare. Sometimes he played to her, sat her on his knee at the piano and, growling in the bass, taught her the nursery rhymes that made her laugh. Mamma's language was different. She read stories at bedtime: Cenerentola, about the girl at home among the ashes, or Pinocchio, the boy whose jointed wooden bones were carved in a workshop and whose nose was as long as the lies he told. But English came later, from her father, and it came in songs with queer rhyming repeats, like 'Mary, Mary, quite contrary' or 'incy wincy spider'.

When they arrived at the playground it was clear that something was wrong: the swings had gone. No, they hadn't gone; they were all looped up, twisted round their metal scaffolds and tied with chains. Where they should have hung was a great empty space, purposeless and blank. The small roundabout also had a chain across it, like a beast being restrained. All the swoop and thrill of the place had gone, set beyond bounds. She stood and stared, the disappointment so intense she was struck dumb. 'What is it?' she whispered, as if she needed to be careful, as if a cataclysm had come and wrecked the place and might return at any time. For a moment her father seemed equally at a loss. Then, shrugging, he remembered: 'Oh, it's Sunday—the Sabbath. Never mind. You can come another day.'

But this day, the one that she had, the one that now loomed endless and purposeless into the distance, would never come again. It had been snatched from her by some freak of denial and by a word she didn't wholly understand: Sabbath. The immeasurable sadness of walking home again under the disapproving Edinburgh tenements, the afternoon deranged, her playtime unplayed, was like grief for a lost time. 'Non c'è?' she asked, bewildered still and lapsing into Italian. What was it, exactly? Something more than a swing's lovely game of scuff and go, push and pull. She turned to look back at the empty triangles, hollowed through where the inviting seats might have hung. But he tugged her away, impatient now, preoccupied with other things. 'Never mind', he repeated, explaining nothing. 'We'll come another day.'

Life from Sixteen Angles

On the return, as they walked past the biscuit factory with its gloomy flat facade, its high chimneys and barred darkened windows, she suddenly thought she saw it, that thing she met in her dreams sometimes, waking terrified though never quite sure why: the shape of a monkey sitting at a window. She shrank and whimpered, even while knowing that dreams didn't cross into real life and that, however much she disliked the grim, dilapidated building which she always passed on the way to the swings, there were no monkeys inside.

'Let's sing', he said suddenly, perhaps only to stop her dragging her feet. He started humming under his breath, humming till she remembered the words and joined in: 'He marched them up to the top of the hill, and he marched them down again.' And then suddenly, for no reason, it was funny, marching there and marching back, and she started to swing his arm to the beat, up and down, up and down, stepping in time to his long steps as they marched back down imaginary hills.

3—Piano Houses

Once they removed the strong, five-barred wooden gate at the top of the stairs, through which she could only peer into the darkness, her passage was opened. A black-and-green striped carpet pointed the way, arrowing over each high step, lower and lower to the basement below. She soon learned to manoeuvre downwards, sitting on each step as she went and shuffling forwards till her feet met the next. His room was in the basement, next to the scullery with its horrible square tub and mangling rollers. That was Mamma's room, where each week the washing was done, rollered into stiff, half-human shapes and pegged out to dry. The washing line in the garden would then carry a row of grotesque self-effigies, a whole waving family of shirts and skirts and trousers to be whisked and beaten by the wind. Mamma always did the washing on a Sunday, until one of the neighbours came knocking on the door to say: did she not know what day it was? Not even clothes were allowed to swing on a Sunday.

But next door was her father's room. From there, the house was filled with noises—not tunes, like the ones he taught her to sing, but odd, contorted twists of noise which he repeated and repeated, like someone hammering a point home till it arrived—and then there was suddenly quiet. Once, when the front of the piano had been removed, he let her sit there while he worked, and she saw how rows of woolly hammers jerked up and down, like her knees when tapped by the doctor, and how the strings had tiny patches of cloth on them, and how they hung, some in one direction, some in another, knotted at each end with a pin. His feet worked the pedals up and down, up and down, making the sound bigger and longer, while his fingers crouched and danced on the white keys. Then he'd stop and play for her, very loudly and full of notes so it was not quite right, not as Nanny used to play it, but as if he was making a joke: *O-o-o-h, Hokey Cokey Cokey*, and she would waggle her fingers from head to toe, laughing fit to burst. The wooden contraption, jumping to attention at the touch of his hands, rippled and thumped, its hundreds of articulated wooden rods rolling in waves. It was like Pinocchio, she thought, all bits of this and that, hammers and strings, rods and pins—stuff from a carpenter's workshop—and somehow a dead thing till, suddenly, in his hands, it came alive.

She started piano lessons when she was six. Her teacher, Miss Lovell, seemed very old; she lived in a large gloomy house with a grand piano in the sitting room, and always wore a round fur hat, a woollen jacket and gloves which were cut off at the fingers. She had a round face and no neck, and was altogether like a round furry animal, curled into a ball against the cold—a cold which those large, unheated Edinburgh houses harboured for months. In winter, she and her younger brother had itchy red chilblains which swelled their toes out of shape and pressed against their shoes. They wore woollen gloves that became soaked in rain or snow, and gave off curious, sheepish smells. When they rolled snowmen in the back garden, their gloves would clot, snow clinging like webbing between their fingers, till it melted and left their hands numb.

Miss Lovell's woollen half-gloves would walk over the white keys as she explained the names of the notes: the ones in Granny's house, round the note G, and the ones in Daddy's house, round the note D. Each had a roof of black keys and a floor of white keys. Granny's was bigger. Out of those two houses came her first tunes: three blind mice, which went one way, downwards, and Frère Jacques which went the other way, upwards. A note to each finger, she had to make her own small hands cup over those mice so that they ran, or wake Frère Jacques from his sleep. She could hear them in her head, how they should go, but her fingers wouldn't always catch them.

Notes, she thought, were strange things: they were only bits of wood and wool knocking together inside a piano, just as she was only bits of bone knocking inside her flesh. But then they were also, sometimes, a tune that flew about the room, that could make you laugh or cry, or make your heart stop still for the sheer thrill of it. Miss Lovell, when she stopped the lesson to play to her, could let the notes fly out of their ivory houses and live like creatures that had suddenly found their souls. Then the piano came alive, and although you could see nothing but the same shabby room, with its sunken sofa, its doily-covered table, its fringed standing lamp, it was filled with the wings of an angel about to fly.

4—Doubles

She, was it? or was it already *I?* At what point do we start to fit our pronouns, fill our allotted roles, take our accidental places in the world? Or do we, perhaps, always double up—*she,* the wondering, watching child, always hidden in *I,* who adapts to the world? *she,* the unplaced, inarticulate one, hidden in *I,* with a language and a nationality? Like everyone else, I was born in a place—a place that would be stamped on my passport forever, giving me my rights of habitation and language, my wider entitlements of pride or shame. That place happened to be the same as my father's: Wakefield, England. But it was crossed at the start by another, courtesy of my Neapolitan mother, whose language was my first and whose landscape lent itself to other myths and manners.

Across those two, English / Italian, Anglo-Saxon / Latin, millstone grit / Vesuvian lava, there were others which would complicate my outlook on the world: my father's music on the one hand, my mother's relaxed Catholicism on the other; my father's shy working-class beginnings, my mother's complex regional inferiorities. Scotland, where we landed, had its own varieties of inclusion and antagonism, its own unpredictable complexities of difference. 'Go home, Sassenachs!' the rolling, not unfriendly drunk bawled at our backs as we walked, my father and I, down Princes Street that first year in the new city. 'Fuck the Pope', the boys chanted at the bus-stop where I stood uncomfortably hung in my convent uniform. 'Pray for the Holy Father', the Irish nuns lilted at morning assembly. 'The Pope's a rogue and a scoundrel', my Italian Nonno growled, regaling his amazed granddaughter with sensational examples of church corruption, while not disdaining to show me, deep in his wallet, some reliquary petals of Santa Rosa which he kept in case of need. When, once, I was accosted in the playground by a woman who asked, accusingly, bafflingly: 'Are you Jewish?' it was part of the same syndrome of discomfort. Many years later, the London pub owner who, during the Falklands crisis, greeted me with: 'We don't serve Argentinians in here', was only one in a line of those who, when they looked, saw something not quite indigenous.

Foreignness was there at the beginning, a criss-crossing of languages, purposes, expectations, which was then reinforced as the norm at my convent school. Aged six, I failed to enter any of the classier Merchant schools of Edinburgh; I simply failed the exams they set: curious mathematical puzzles disguised as games. So I was sent to the Catholic convent of the Sacred Heart, at Craiglockhart. It was a day school that took all sorts, though boys were only accepted in class one, and only if, in deference to the coded femininity of the place, they wore kilts. Alongside a number of Scots, my class contained a Nigerian, two Pakistani Muslims, a couple of English Anglicans, a good number of Italians and Irish, and one seriously disturbed girl who might otherwise have been in a special school, and whose inarticulate calls and habits of suddenly taking all her clothes off, were tolerated alongside everyone else's peculiarities. Varieties of foreignness marked us, alongside a faith which made a point of never being totally at home.

Throughout my eight years at the convent, aged six to fourteen, I never knew that the building had been a war hospital, housing shell-shocked soldiers from the First World War, including Owen and Sassoon. They must have walked the same long, gloomy corridors of the old building, with its parquet floors and closed-off rooms. Now those corridors were brightened by Catholic soft kitsch: kindly, colourful statues which opened their arms to us, as if our destination was to be forever embraced. They gentled the long passageways and enlivened dark corners. Spiritual guardians who peopled our child's world, overseers of our small woes or fears, their role was to answer all prayers and invocations: St Vincent de Paul for sickness, St Ursula for help in learning, St Jude for lost causes. We might never be alone in those paths, where we filed in procession each week and every feast day to the chapel at the far end. But that darker presences haunted the place, or that cries and screams once rang out in the night, was not part of our history. We were the children of easier times.

As the sixties brought their liberations and temptations, we learned to play double. We knew how to curtsey politely to the Reverend Mother while continuing to walk, we wore tunics to our knees and modesty knickers beneath our gym shorts; each day, at noon, we stopped whatever lesson we were doing to recite the Angelus. At some level we accepted the dramas of salvation and damnation that were everywhere around us, expressed in the decor and decorum of the place. At the same time, with the Beatles keening in our bloodstream, we learned to hitch up our tunics at the gates of the school, to cadge for wolf whistles in the street, to cross our legs and smoke cigarettes in the Wimpey Bars. If, on the one hand, we were prepared to stand with our arms outstretched in chapel on Good Friday, moved almost to tears, we were also learning to scrutinise that ubiquitous, near-naked body which hung in all our classrooms: the tendons of the stretched armpits, the numbered rods of the ribs, the twisted feet, and the small kink of the groin as it dipped behind the loin cloth. Our education in faith turned effortlessly into an education in the erotic. We trooped to chapel just the same, while Vatican Two turned Latin to English, rote catechism to debate, old absolutes to new interpretations. But our bodies were registering the thrilling possibilities of life outside, where old rules were breaking down and old assumptions being challenged. If the convent protected us from its past, it could not protect us from our own present.

Meanwhile, we learned to swim in the basement pool—the pool where Owen and Sassoon had probably swum before, to ease mental and physical scars that we could never imagine. The same cubicles, showing head and feet but hiding the parts between, might have served them also for modesty. The same rectangle of green water, that accepted our pubescent bodies, embraced their scarred, memory-haunted limbs. Ours was the world that came after, and Craiglockhart, with its wide views across the city, its large grounds marked by courts and shrines, its benign rituals of salvation, flowers, candles, white frocks and veils, succeeded, as did much of the 1960s and 70s, in covering the traces of its past. But somewhere in those walls and floors, in the honeyed smell of beeswax and incense, Madonna lilies and school dinners, the place retained its stony knowledge of other lives and fates.

5—Cross Stitch

Mother McGory picked up a bobbin of yellow thread, pointedly drew it out to measure, then quickly cut it short. She squinted close as she drew it, slowly, through the eye of a needle. It seemed to take an eternity and the class waited in bored silence. Last week, chain stitch; this week, cross stitch; next, feather stitch. Mother McGory taught needlework and Christian doctrine, a combination that reflected, not only their combined lowly status, as we surmised, but also their similarities. Catechism classes were originally taught, like embroidery, line by line, week by week, from a book called *The Light of the World*. Our class of seven-year-olds learned by heart the answers to such questions as: *'Who is God?' 'Has God a Body?' 'Where is God?'* and were required to give word-perfect answers that seemed, very often, only more mysterious: 'God is the Supreme Spirit who alone exists of Himself and is infinitely perfect.' 'God has no body, He is a pure spirit.' 'God is everywhere.' Sometimes we recited the answers in unison, sometimes individually. If mistakes were made Mother McGory tutted loudly and repeated the question till someone answered correctly. Since by the age of seven we had already learned the Latin Mass by heart, these philosophical conundrums were only another translatable language for the mystery that surrounded us on all sides. Metaphor was the air we breathed.

But metaphor flourishes best where it is not grounded, and the convent gave us a world in which translatability rarely settled into empirical fact. Innumerable statues of 'the Sacred Heart', for instance, were meant to represent the very heart of the place; but those curious anatomical glory holes, where a bright red flame glowed within the exposed area of a man's chest, only sent the name ricocheting back into metaphor again. A Sacred Heart was not exactly a heart, not exactly a man, not exactly a statue of a man, not exactly a God-made-man, but something in the process of constantly metonymising from one to the other, like a line of poetry. For all our rote learning, the languages we juggled—English, Latin, metaphysical, metonymical, sculptural, tactile—kept their magic of wonder and transposition. 'O Sacred Heart, Our home lies deep in thee', we sang in chapel, untroubled by the mix of anatomical, erotic, metaphorical and literal presence it held together. Home was like that anyway—an endlessly relocated destination. However, we learned very early that, in order not to antagonise those outside the gates, the question 'What school do you go to?' was better answered by 'Craiglockhart' than 'Convent of the Sacred Heart'. Sacred Hearts were liable to rouse, in the uninitiated, puzzled antagonism, if not verbal abuse.

It was no surprise, then, that cross stitch too might be another link in a world that stretched out metaphorically in all directions. Mother McGory, hunched and wizened as she was, would lift up her square of green baize and begin her row of identical stitches while, one by one, we took turns to stand beside her and watch. There was a queer purposeless point to it, like so much that we learned at the convent. Questions of relevance or significance did not figure. We learned to measure and knot the thread, to write our lines of meaningless Xs, without ever asking what it could profit us in a world beckoning with more thrilling temptations. For cross stitch, like everything else in the place, was written into a map of the universe created for the greater glory of God. We learned to embroider for the sake of it, making rows of stitches that went nowhere and meant nothing, while at the same time learning to embroider in the language itself, tracing the links that ran, sometimes wildly, between this world and others. Mother McGory, her nature impressed with the grim intimations of her name, presided like some ancient Fate over our small endeavours in the art of the useless.

The bad girl of the class—the one who would later rebel against the rules by being too free with the boys and having to leave when she became pregnant—one day, waiting bored at the nun's side, took a tiny snip of the hem of her veil, just above the shoulder. It was barely an inch, but the rest of us watched with fascination. After that, week after week, we checked to see if the tiny breach had been mended. But no, either Mother McGory was too short-sighted, or too busy with other thoughts. The tiny cut remained where it was, and embroidery lessons, with their rote of artless elaboration, continued as before.

Like all the nuns, Mother McGory smelled of soap and slightly musty habit. Her veil was attached to a ruched headpiece which framed her face and hid all her hair. Her eyes were deep-set and lacklustre, her body bowed and her temper short. She seemed to us ancient as the hills, a figure of mystery and ugliness, whose granite-like countenance rarely showed any expression beyond the frown of so many wrinkles. Cross stitch, she reminded us once, in a moment of rare disclosure, should make us think of the crosses we had to bear, and we should offer them up to the Lord who had travelled his own Stations of the Cross. Thus another word took off on its journey into space, where it joined strange constellations of sense beyond the gravities of fact. It seemed appropriate that Mother McGory, so taciturn and cross a figure herself, should show us, without any wit or humour, another small shooting star in the sky of our language. Meanwhile, she plied her needle undisturbed, making rows of little yellow kisses on that frayed green baize.

✝

When Mother McGory died some years later, we all filed to the chapel for the Requiem Mass. She was laid out in sombre state in her coffin, looking almost statuesque, larger than life now that life no longer bowed her down. There she lay, flowers at her head and feet, hands clasped across her chest, the silver crucifix at her heart. We processed slowly past 'to pay our last respects'—a phrase that never quite translated into either a prayer or a proper goodbye. She lay in the old habit we knew, the white ruff circling her familiar creased face, her veil stretched taut on either side, her thick black shoes a little unrealistically propped upright. We filed round her, uncertain what we should do or think, for once not curtseying or bowing, just looking, curiously. She had gone to the destination that was the focal point of everything we learned and to which the sweet-faced statues forever beckoned. But she took with her on her last journey, visible to none but ourselves, that tiny snip in her veil, still unmended by any of the stitches she had so patiently taught us. It was the smallest breach, but it held our attention like a flaw that nothing, perhaps, would put right.

6—Night Train

Edinburgh to King's Cross, King's Cross to Victoria, Victoria to Dover, Dover to Calais, Calais to Rome, Rome to Naples—for three interminable days, skies clearing and the world warming, the ratchet heart of a train turned over and over beneath our feet. Only the Channel crossing changed that rote, the rhythm of the sea improvising wildly, jostling or level, rough or smooth. Slipping loose from moorings at Dover, with the cliffs raw and white above us, the sea accepting us into its sway, became a yearly escape that divided our loyalties and forked our tongues. Landscapes and languages altered as we went, green rolling fields giving way to brown hills, Anglo-Saxon consonants to Latin vowels. That journey, repeated summer after summer every year of our childhood, was like a crossing between the poles of our lives, from north to south, cool to warm, English to Italian. At Calais, we nervously crossed the gap between platform and train—a gap that opened onto a hissing metallic underworld, a grinding machinery of shafts and cogs and locks that would tread us slowly southwards. The compartment into which we climbed would then carry us for two more days, in the company of strangers, almost to the house by the volcano. It contained a little formica table that jutted out from the window, a metal ashtray with a clattery lid, and sagging baggage nets above our heads. *Non gettare alcun oggetto dal finestrino*—like a mesmerising tune, the line would sing us back into the mother tongue.

For three days we travelled to the other place with Mamma. Kenneth stayed at home to compose. So for three days we half-dreamed, half-dozed, while the dull catch and lilt of the wheels clocked up miles and miles of land. A world rolled past that was always changing. There were trees, fields, houses, hills; then trees turning darker, fields smaller, houses taller, hills higher. Telegraph poles scanned our passing, marking time: one, then another, then another, faster or slower. There was nothing to do but sit and watch, an ordeal of weariness and boredom which was also an education in doing nothing. We had no games, no books even, and the place was too public for our secret silliness and childhood conspiracies. Instead, we were limited to a choice of windows: the one in the carriage or the one in the corridor, to sitting or standing, standing or sitting. Reluctantly, from time to time, we took the crowded, rocking route down to the stinky lavatory at the end of the corridor where, between our legs, we watched open ground rush by in a sucking draught. Otherwise, when not fretting for a drink or a snack, we day-dreamed, hour after hour, watching and hearing a world timed by the transience of our passage, and the rotary repetitions of the wheels.

Life from Sixteen Angles

Stations, at least, were an alleviation, with their crowds stranded in islands of baggage, or running, shouting, sending last messages —then, when there was no more to be said, waving, waving, waving. Sometimes, however, stations were deserted and silent, and we seemed to wait an eternity for no reason, the station clock ticking slowly and the heat building in our airless compartments. Then we were desperate, lost in a world of purposeless immobility, homesick to be gone. Without the companionable churn of the wheels, our conversations were exposed and vulnerable, their banalities lapsing quickly into quiet. The agony of those interminable pauses at least confirmed for us, poor trapped creatures, that movement, change, passage were our natural condition. When the train eventually re-engaged with a thump, hauling out of the empty enclosure, the air circulating so we could breathe again, it was as if we'd been given a reprieve of our lives.

Meanwhile, however, through the long monotonous hours, we were adapting to the changes: to landscapes in different colours, hills that surprised our horizons, altering skies. Above all, we were adapting to a language which welled up from the depths of consciousness, almost from the womb, and which dictated its own differences of accent, volume, intention. We thought we were watching the world go by. In fact, we were attending to a world coming in.

✂

Many years later, covering the same ground, I suddenly opened my eyes and remembered how it always was. The sheet was stiff and raw under my chin, the hairy blanket had rucked down to my feet. Cautiously I sat up and, feeling the cold, drew back again. Two straps reached to the ceiling, belting me into the top bunk. I could see the blue night-light at the far end and, below, the dim forms of other sleepers. The train was tilting rhythmically from side to side, making the leather blind tap against the window. I lay for a while, hearing the quiet all round, and that one sound, *tap-tap, tap-tap*, repeating over and over like the wings of a moth trying to get in. Then I rose up on one elbow and peered out.

The air was clear as an angel. I could make out a jigsaw of peaks and sky, fitting together in an unearthly match. Alps of the heart, I thought, quoting something that I couldn't remember. That great cut across the night, a selvage of stone and snow, was familiar, magical, a divide that still seemed impossible to cross. Yet I had come through it many times in my life: the night, the cold, that hush of wide white space crossing the path of my journey. The man in the bunk below turned over heavily and sighed. The train slowed to a crawl, wary and uncertain, as if feeling huge obstacles in its way—and out there, the mountains that cut Europe in half, delivering its weathers on both sides, calling its travellers to attention. The train freewheeled for a time, audibly slowing, then simply stopped. Everything emptied into quiet, into that high strained noiselessness in which the breathing of my fellow travellers was like the last sound on earth. I could see in my mind's eye the long line of the train, with its neatly stacked cargo of sleepers shelved three to a wall, each dreaming separately against the suspended, irrelevant space outside. My nerves prickled with apprehension, and I fell to wondering if the train had broken down, if there was something on the line, if one of those high banks of snow had come crashing down.

But no, it was only the approach to a station. The train jerked slowly forward, then slid quietly in and stopped again. There was a voice on the platform, a step, then silence. I caught sight of a man in uniform, a hip, the holster of a gun. Of course, I remembered, this was the border, the invisible line between here and there, one country and another. There's always a line, scored in tongues, nourished by blood, manned by guards. This is one country, that another; ours, theirs; mine, yours. I lay listening to that eerie prelude of quiet, the sound of the breathing sleepers so near me, the high silence of the snow-covered mountains, while knowing that any minute the interruption would come.

And indeed, suddenly there it was: a loud knock. The compartment door was drawn back, and a shock of wakening light came in. The guard, looking over his shoulder, trumpeted loud enough to wake the dead: '*passaporti, tutti i passaporti, biglietti.*' The other sleepers groaned and cursed, rubbing their eyes, struggling to find papers in the cramped disorder of bunks in which they had half undressed. Mine was ready, to hand. I knew this rough interruption from childhood: the way he would come in, unannounced, unexpected, breaking the privacy of our dreams, demanding papers in the strong bare light. It was a check, reminiscent of others in other countries, the light breaking in on small cramped places, prisons or hideaways, the culprits exposed. I also knew that momentary panic, the sense of not quite inhabiting oneself, fearing some mismatch. Handing over my blue and gold passport, I held my breath as he flipped the pages, puzzled over place-names long ago allotted me, scrutinised the photo. Once again, I was crossing the invisible line which scored through my life, leaving me often uncertain, either side of it. Was something not in order? Could I be other? Outside the window, those eerie pinnacles lifted indifferently into the night sky.

Life from Sixteen Angles

It seemed an age before the train moved on, lurching forward, then engaging, till it eased into its old rhythm and the blind started to beat again on the window, and the great dream spaces stepped back to let us pass. In relief and exhaustion I dozed off for a short while. What woke me next was the whammy of a tunnel. We must have entered at speed, and I felt the shudder of it all down the carriage, my ears popping with the compression of air. It was a tight squeeze, this tunnelling below mountains of rock, heights of snow, as the train wormed through the barrier of the Alps. This was, I realised, as deep as I'd ever be, alive. Above were thousands of feet of stone, the weight of them held off by a small brick tunnel. How long could we last under there, if we had to stop? But the train was rushing through with a high-pitched whine, shaking and rattling to the tunnel's brick retort. Only when it broke into the open again did the sound relax, and a quieter rhythm cradled me back to sleep.

The sun, when I awoke, was storming the edges of the blind, striking a warm shaft across my chest. I could hear voices in the corridor. The train was running smoothly, the suspense and effort of the night all passed. I had come through, it seemed, as so often, once more. The heat increased as we slipped through Italy. Sometimes the train stopped, nowhere, for no reason, hard by a field where cicadas fidgeted, sea-sawing between two notes. In the quiet I might hear the buzz of conversation, a rumour which the wheels had suppressed but which now grew loud like the swell of discontent. The burly man opposite puffed out his cheeks in annoyance at each stop: '*uffa!*' he expostulated, putting his head out of the window. *Non gettare alcun oggetto* . . . But there was only the same sizzling quiet outside, and the silver lines heading into the distance.

The roads to Rome, I thought. I had learned their names in Latin lessons with the nuns: Aurelian, Appian, Domitian. They went out like spokes of a wheel, arteries from a heart. One of them was permanently mapped in my blood . . . and for a moment I saw, somewhere else at the far end of it, the great knuckle of rock overlooking the North Sea at the Roman station of Ravenscar. It was grey with one of those hangovers of mist that turn the air to wet wool on a summer's day. I had gone there with Kenneth. As we approached the coast, the sun had misted over till there was nothing but purple-grey, a fret like an army of ghosts creeping inland. The road to Rome, I thought, lay behind my life in a great swathe of history and chance. I looked at my watch. Not long now. The train seemed to be hurtling full-tilt to its destination, like a beast smelling home. It careered past fields of yellow sunflowers, peaked hilltop villages, straggling modern towns on the plains. But instead of watching and waiting that last hour or so, I fell asleep again. It was as if the old summer heat of the siesta was insisting on its rights. My body was clocking into its other time. And I dreamed I was walking in an English park. There were red squirrels scurrying up and down the trees, like the ones I remembered from childhood in Yorkshire. One stopped on its hind legs and unwrapped a nut, fast as a party trick, watching me all the while. But I could not stop; I had a child by the hand. She whimpered and stumbled, trying to keep up. It seemed we would never get to our destination. I pulled her harder, but her legs were too short and she lagged back. I looked down, wondering how I had come to be responsible for such a small creature, thinking I might shake her off and go on alone. But then I saw her face, and it was myself, looking up, breathless, holding on to Mamma who was saying: 'Be quick, you must run. We must catch the train home. *Andiamo presto!*'

⅄

When I woke, it was to the sound of people stretching and chattering, fetching down their suitcases. The hypnotic rote of the wheels had slackened. Outside, a broken aqueduct trailed across the waste land. A square terraced farmhouse with an old stone courtyard slid slowly past. Then the view crowded. Blocks of modern flats, the colourful plaster peeling in great scabs, hugged round the train. The city was closing in. The old journey home was reaching its destination. And once again, as so many times before, I prepared to tune in to the new speech, the altered perspectives, the sense of difference colouring a world under the same sun.

7—Bone-Lace

'Where's Gina?

That was always our first question when we arrived. We never thought about her much at other times of the year—never during the long months away, in another country, nor on the slow train journey back, waking on the third day, our ears still full of the slam of tunnels, feeling the new soft-pedal of the sun; nor, later, in Rome, changing from a stale, crumb-ridden compartment to a new train for Naples; nor even later, on the little wood-slatted Vesuviana, which lurched mulishly out of the bay, past the stinking flames of the petro-chemicals, and on through strips of market gardening towards San Giorgio at the foot of the volcano. But as soon as we arrived at the Villa Madonnina, even before the first embraces were over, we'd be clamouring:

'Where's Gina?'

Gina had black hair, temple-streaked with grey, tied back in a bun. Her eyes were even blacker, sharp as a rat's, and creased into fixed smiles by the wrinkles of her face. She had a whiskery moustache which tickled when she kissed us, and a body that smelled of kitchen and working sweat. Gina was Sicilian, but had lived with the family for as long as I could remember. Hers was the room at the back of the kitchen, more cupboard than room, with space only for a brass-headed bed, a chest of drawers and a wickerwork chair. On the chest was a photograph of her husband Vittorio. He gazed out thoughtfully from the curly fanfare of a gilt-edged frame, topped with a black bow. Beribboned and sad, he looked like a lonely child at a party. When Gina was not in the kitchen, elbow deep at the sink or stirring a pan of spaghetti on the stove, we found her sitting in her room, working her beaded bobbins of lace. They hung on fine threads from a huge, barrel-shaped, horsehair bolster. Rough hairs poked through between the threads like something human half-bundled out of sight. Sometimes, but only if she was in a good humour, she would let us in and we crept onto the bed, carefully, so as not to disturb her bobbins with their delicately spreading wing of lace.

Gina knew things that nobody else did or that nobody would tell us. She knew about the gardener's boy who was up to no good in Naples at the weekend; she knew about the latest Camorrista murder down in the olive grove outside the village; about abductions and thefts, eruptions and bad harvests and the Liquefaction of Blood. She didn't have any regard for childhood. She told us facts not stories, innocently and at random, without warning or explanation. But facts in her mouth had the ring of stories, and Gina's disclosures were our entry to the place: its beauty and terror, its fierce weathers and intimate violence. We were flattered and spell-bound. No one else offered us a glimpse of the real world with such a free hand.

Once, after shopping, she took us to see the *ex votos* in her church. They were the best in Italy, she assured us proudly. As for the church, it was the most beautiful in the world. At first we saw nothing in the dim side-chapel except a huge, brocaded, white and blue Madonna. But Gina was looking at something else. Gradually we realised that all three walls were barnacled with things, like an underwater cave. There were fat silver hearts studded with jewels, wax arms and legs like the broken limbs of dolls, an old shoe, a thick plait of chestnut hair, a picture of a stick-man falling off a ladder, another of Vesuvius erupting in flames, and everywhere, vague brown shapes in moulded wax, too dingy to name. We shifted awkwardly before that motley, pitiful collection of trophies. Like Gina's own stories, it was not the evidence of the miraculous that struck us, but the bald, ordinary matter of fact: that someone had cut off her beautiful hair, or broken an arm, or fallen off a ladder. Reality's artless, ill-assorted accidents took shape before our eyes in those intimately exposed parts, those frank fragments. Above it all, the Madonna, with her pink cheeks and painted eye-liner, held out hopelessly helping hands. We stood silently by as Gina muttered some prayers, then kissed her knuckles close to her chest. On the way home she showed us how to guard against the evil eye.

That summer the heat seemed to crack open the air. Each day, by mid-morning, the sky had deepened to a dusty blue and the cicadas seemed to rub thousands of hands in the trees above our heads. They turned up the volume of the quiet to a sawing obsession, like a disturbance of the nerves. The air contracted till it became hard to breathe. Heat sprang at us from the terra-cotta urns of the terrace and the crazy paving of the paths. It laid burning hands on our arms and legs, and bit our fingers from the railing round the fishpond. Above it all, on the near horizon, hung the charred, grainy-red wedge of Vesuvius, a spiral of white smoke curling from the top like an old trick that deceives no one. Tilted like the profile of a face, angular, dreamy, it caught us out in our moments of boredom, crossed our minds, stalked the field of our childhood vision. Half-consciously we watched it, glancing up from our invented games to check its stillness, its silent, upturned, wide open mouth, its look of awful unfinished concentration.

And so we often took refuge with Gina. Her room on the ground floor was cooler than most and, unlike everyone else, she was rarely asleep in the afternoons. We would climb onto the bed and listen to her talk, half to us, half to herself, as she shuttled her bobbins from hand to hand, twisting and crossing the white threads. 'Poor Vittorio,' she muttered from time to time, tapping his photograph and blowing him a kiss. The dead, like children, were brought into her conversations naturally, without any special invitation. Gina kept open house to whatever came to mind.

One day she announced, suddenly, as if she'd just remembered: 'I saw him you know, my poor Vittorio.' We were stung with interest. How could she have seen him? He had been dead for years. Did she mean a ghost? But Gina's stories did not often go our way. 'Of course not!' she exclaimed, disdainful and offended. She fell silent, and we waited. She rarely dropped hints without taking them up again, like the spidery stitches of her fine white lace which grew, wing by wing, into a perceptible pattern, and then eventually into something useful and simple, like a collar, a handkerchief or a hem for a petticoat. But she pressed her lips together as if determined that, this time, nothing should get through, and worked her bobbins with renewed energy. They clattered together as she plaited them in pairs, deftly driving a long brass pin through each spread-eagled stitch as it appeared. *Click click, click click.* Those light wooden spindles rattled in the background of all her stories, a rough continuo to all their inconsequence, halts and surprises. We waited in hope. Vittorio also waited, patiently, in his frame.

Eventually Gina shrugged, and pursued her own line of thought. 'When I saw Vittorio, it was him all right.' 'Unmistakable!' she added after a pause, with a hint of triumph. We huddled a little closer together on the bed.

'How did you know?' my brother whispered. She snorted for a reply. 'Where was it?' he urged, looking uneasily about. 'Was it here?'

'Of course not, stupid! How could it be here? He was up at the cemetery.'

The obviousness of it took the wind out of our sails. The bobbins rattled on through our silence, unembarrassed, and she continued: 'He's been dead nine years, nine years last April. Poor Vittorio.' We waited respectfully, but she seemed to have finished and was tutting anxiously at the lace before her. Something had gone wrong with one of her stitches. Sighing, she unpicked it, lifting four bobbins gently up and down, keeping the pin tightly between her lips. When she'd eased it back, I picked up my courage: 'Where exactly did you see him when you saw him?' My voice was hushed with prepared mystification. Gina's was not. 'Up at the cemetery as I said,' she retorted, 'with the keeper of skeletons.'

Before we had time to rescue our thoughts from their scared hideouts, she had launched into a kind of explanation:

'And those were the trousers I'd bought him, just the same! It seemed like yesterday that I'd laid him out. Still . . .' she paused: 'I'd have known him anywhere.' She glanced at the photograph apologetically. 'They go quite brown and dry in there. It's the lava. It pickles you well and truly.' Her eyes filled for a moment and she blew her nose. Gina's emotions were always unpredictable. Outside, the peaked, charred mountain stayed silent—tinder to set the sky alight. 'To think it's as long as nine years', she murmured.

At this she fell into silent musing. We were glad of it on the whole, for we were still trying to piece together what she'd told us. Poor Vittorio had been rolled out before us in a form we couldn't make head nor tail of. Expecting to encounter spooks and spectres, we were bewildered by this dry, literal encounter, clicky with its bare bones of fact. 'What happened next?' my brother grumbled. Then brightening with a good idea of his own, asked: 'Did it *move*?' But Gina remained immovable in her truth:

'Of course it didn't move. The dead don't move, do they? They just lie still. They cleaned him up, though, polished his old bones like any worn furniture. I'd thought, before, it was a shame to shift them, drag them out of the earth so soon, just when they'd got settled. But then, when I saw him, I thought: that's all right. It makes space for others.' She gazed thoughtfully round the room. Then slowly, she began to pack up her bobbins, pinning them to the bolster with strips of cloth so they didn't get mixed up. 'But of course,' she reflected, 'what with being knocked about like that, he started to come apart. The joins had gone. They had to fold him up. Like a clothes-horse,' she snapped.

I wondered, anxiously, what my nuns would have made of this. 'She's with Our Lord,' they sing-songed cheerfully when old Mother McGory died and they laid her out for the Requiem Mass. But Gina's version gripped me. It was sharp and practical, handy as a manual, with nothing in it to make you either good or bad, frightened or cheerful. I glanced at Vittorio in his curly gilt frame that spread out like a halo. He looked, somehow, resigned – not frightened or cheerful, either.

'What happened next?'

'They wrapped him up in a white cloth,' she explained. 'The poor bones rattled together as they moved, light as dry sticks.' She shrugged imperceptibly. 'Then they shut him in a drawer, all polished and shiny. His photo's on the front', she added like an afterthought, and nodded towards the chest, as if to reassure the original that it was indeed the same. I was puzzled about the photograph. But I had to admit, everything else hung together. There was Vittorio, tucked away for the Last Day, packed and

Life from Sixteen Angles

labelled like any other luggage. I looked at Gina with admiration. She was folding up her bobbins in a small white napkin. They rattled against each other in a conversational sort of way, as if they'd been waiting to put their heads together.

Suddenly a voice came loudly from the kitchen: *'Gina! Vieni qui!'* She looked at her watch and shooed us quickly out. We were wasting her time and she had better things to do. So we returned to the garden, where the red geraniums flamed in their terracotta urns, a swallowtail flopped like a shuttlecock over them, and everywhere the cicadas sharpened their small knives in the heat of the day. Beyond the garden, an alley of oleanders led down and out, past the Madonnina herself in a blue and white ceramic plaque, mooning over a smiling baby. And beyond the oleanders, through a wooden gate, a grove of stricken, ancient olives, gnarled and twisted, belonged to the other country—the one that lies always just on the far side, however sharply you draw the line or erect a frontier. The Madonnina was our limit that summer. Beyond her we were not allowed to go.

Some days later we found our way back to Gina's room. It was too hot to play and our imaginations flagged. To our surprise we found a large package on the bed. Gina was tidying things away in the chest of drawers, her hands gesticulating nervously as she moved. She seemed to be carrying on an argument with her hands, which proposed first one thing, then another, paused, changed tack, made a further suggestion, in a queer passionate dumb-show of decisions.

'What are you doing?' we demanded to know. She stopped in her tracks for a moment, prevaricating. It was a hopeful sign and we settled side by side on the bed.

'What's this?' I asked, tapping the package. She paused before replying. Then, as she always did, answered our questions with a new kind of knowledge. 'Do you want to see?' Her eyes sparkled with excitement and her voice couldn't wait.

'Of course!' we chorused.

She dragged the package onto her knees and opened it carefully, almost lovingly. We wondered what Gina could have bought that was so big. Her room, like her eyes, almost couldn't contain it. Then, to our astonishment, she drew out of the tissue, rustling darkly, a long black dress, quite plain and smooth, with wide cuffed sleeves and buttons to the neck.

'It's a dress!' I confirmed. What could Gina want with a new dress? I thought. She always wore old ones, mostly invisible under her aprons.

'It's a special dress,' she explained, caressingly. It looked, I thought, special in a way – not grand exactly, not ordinary either. I couldn't make up my mind.

'When will you wear it?' I asked doubtfully. Gina stood up. She held it to her face with one hand, waisted it with the other, and stepped towards us as if about to dance.

'What do you think?' she asked flirtatiously.

'It's beautiful . . .' I paused.

'What's the matter? Don't you like it? Don't you think it suits me?' Her tone was confusing. There was a joke somewhere, but I couldn't find it.

'It's too black,' my brother interjected suddenly, and scrambled off the bed. 'I'm going,' he announced. Dresses were for women and he was pointedly not interested.

'You wouldn't wear it to work,' I considered. 'You never wear dresses like that . . . in the kitchen.' As far as I knew, she had no other place.

'I shall wear it', she answered, suddenly quite serious, 'for a photograph.' She sat down slowly and put the dress to one side. 'A photograph', she repeated, and reached for the bolster of bobbins. Something obscurely made the connection in my mind.

'Like Vittorio's!' I declared, almost before knowing what I meant.

'Of course', she replied, unpinning the strips of cloth so that the bobbins knocked noisily against each other like eager chatterers released from silence. 'This is the most important dress of my life.' I was beginning to understand. Gina had bought a dress for a photo. But not an ordinary photo; it was one like Vittorio's. I considered the original. It looked ordinary enough though rather glum.

'This is the dress I will be buried in,' she explained. 'But first I will have a beautiful photograph. That is the custom. In Sicily, in my village, it is important to buy a dress – a good dress', she emphasised. The idea distressed me. Gina, I realised, had bought a dress to be dead in.

'Why?' I burst out.

'Why what?'

'Why do you need a dress? Or a photograph?

She was evidently mystified. 'So that when they come to visit me at the cemetery, they know who I am, they can say, ah yes, that is certainly her – like I do with Vittorio. It is natural', she concluded. I was still confused.

'Then why don't you wear a blue dress or a red dress? Why don't you have a photo of when you were young, in a party dress or . . .' Gina was shocked.

'That would be quite wrong.' She waved a hand to dispel such notions. 'It must be a serious picture. Only a black dress looks right for death, and an old face', she added. 'Otherwise they will think, she died young, what a pity! It must look sad and ready, as if I were thinking about it in advance. Then, when they look at me,

I will be dead, you see, but in the photograph . . . well, I am not dead yet.' She looked oddly satisfied at this conundrum, as if she'd outwitted someone.

'Then', I shrugged, 'why don't you have a photo of when you are dead? Then it would look like . . . what it looks like.'

'Stupid!' she smiled. 'You don't want to see dead people at the cemetery. You want to have cheerful memories.' I felt hoodwinked again by her seamless logic. 'Anyway,' she reasoned, 'I'm not dead, am I?' She hauled the rustling dress up to her chin and, closing her eyes, pulled a long serious face.

'Don't', I whimpered. 'Don't do that.' I was on the point of tears. This dead-alive dress-rehearsal didn't make any sense. In astonishment Gina caught me up in her arms and held me against her breast. She was essentially soft-hearted and easily moved. 'But it's not real', she crooned. 'It's only a photograph. And the dress is beautiful. Look! Like silk. I'll make a lace collar for it that will be the envy of them all. Your old Gina will look quite stunning at the end. And who', she taunted, 'will know the difference, eh?'

I didn't tell my brother about the dress. He never asked. No one else mentioned it, not even Gina, and in time I also forgot.

The summer passed. Towards the end of August the sky grew tense and heavy with storm. And then, a few days before we were due to depart, it gave birth to a terrifying, melodramatic maniac, who set fire to the trees on the slopes of Vesuvius and crashed senselessly for hours about the sky. The rain beat down upon the earth, seeking entry, then flooded across the fields. The thunder wandered, in shocks and staggers, overhead. Lightning ripped through the massed dark clouds that collected round the tip of the volcano. It felt as if the world were at breaking point. Then, the day after, the temperatures eased, dry leaves blew restlessly about the garden and preparations began for the long journey back. This summer, like all the others, was coming to an end. We would say farewell to the old villa, the pretty fishpond, the alley of oleanders that led down and out, past the Madonnina and through a rickety wooden gate, into the olive grove.

Then we returned slowly north, to the land of shades.

✕

Next summer, when we arrived, we heard the news at once. Poor Gina had died. I remembered in a flash how she'd practised before me, serious yet dancing, solemn yet laughing, and wondered if she'd made the collar of lace. Now her tiny room at the back of the kitchen was stacked full of lumber: ladders, brooms, buckets, boxes of winter clothes and unused china. Nothing of hers remained except the wickerwork chair, which sat in one corner, piled high with blankets. The chest and bed were gone.

Other changes loomed which we didn't understand. The adults whispered secrets to each other, looking meaningful with their eyes. There was talk of moving to a smaller place, perhaps a flat in Naples. Money was tight; there was too much crime. The prospect of leaving edged that last summer with a new sadness. We were growing up. Without Gina we were often bored. The garden seemed smaller and dustier; and the alley of oleanders, leading out to the ominous volcano beyond, seemed short and dull—no longer a path temptingly forbidden.

Yet for one last summer we clung to childhood, playing at playing, now restless and uncertain. One day, among the crates in the back room, we found a box of spillikins. And throughout the long, intemperate afternoons, when the family was asleep and the sun beat down, we played on the cool tiled floor of the kitchen, calling out in the pauses of the sleeping quiet: *'si muove!* it moved!'—the light wooden sticks clattering together in a heap, our eyes and ears keyed to the faintest tremor, as we picked our way among those scattered spindles.

8—In the Music Room

Almost every year they came, and the house filled with presences: those life-sized, human-shaped, closed casks that stood to attention like faceless watchmen. They waited silently, eerie doubles pregnant with purpose. Sometimes, opening on a wine-dark interior, rich as blood and plush with padding, they revealed the inner nut of their husks: a sculptured shape, waisted, curving, notched with two letters that might be *f* or *s*. Tucked into their outlines, perfectly fitting, they contoured the rounds of a body or a sound.

Most years, in the summer, the Wallfischs came to stay. Peter, the pianist, might be giving a concert, or Anita, the cellist, performing with the English Chamber Orchestra. Their son Raphael, who was about my age, was early showing extraordinary musical gifts. I remember those two cellos in their hard cases, standing upright in the music room, waiting for the brush-stroke of a bow.

The sound, when it came, was deep and strange, a sound created by guts and hair, by strings pegged from four wooden ears, strung from the fluted fern of a wood-curl, and drawn taut over a pretty bridge: the ponticello of the cello. Ample and curved, roundy in the depths of itself—from the forest tree that had once been alive, rooting and branching, from the axe-blow that felled it, from the lathe and plane, chisel and hammer that had carved its exact, resonating dimensions—it was a cry I recognised from the start: the stressed tenor of a human voice. At the first note of that sculptured hardwood, I heard a language I fell in love with and wanted to speak. Raphael in time would become a great player, and Kenneth wrote much of his cello music for him. To me, he offered an early instance of that sound, ripe and intimate—a sound drawn from the very fabric of a life, as if from the packed depths of one's own body.

But I took something else away from the music room, besides the seduction of a sound—something harsher, at odds, and perennially incomprehensible. It was summer, and I was sitting next to Anita on the sofa while Peter played the piano. I must have been nine or ten. It was warm and I was restless, and when the music finished I slid to the floor to make my escape. On the way something caught my eye, a small oddity, and with the impulsive curiosity of the child who is still puzzling together pieces of the world, but is not too concerned to hear all the answers, I asked out loud: why have you written numbers on your arm? Anita was a rather formidable person, not inclined to play or laugh, and I think I was struck by the anomaly of her having thus toyed with a pen, as I might have done myself, turning flesh into a memo-pad. At any rate, I didn't wait for the answer, my rhetorical question sufficient, at the time, to the surprise I felt. It was one of those questions no lifetime of knowledge would ever answer. Of course, in time, I learned what the number meant. When many years later I read Anita's book, *Inherit the Truth*, about her time in Auschwitz playing in Alma Rosé's orchestra, I also learned precisely what it was—69388—and how indelible. In that book there is one sentence which, in its appalling curtness, touches on another unimaginable music room—one which might throw all our civilised halls into awful relief, while not giving up on the sound that is made there. At this point she recalls, among the many 'SS personnel who came into our block for light relief', one in particular: 'It was on such an occasion that I played Schumann's *Träumerei* for Dr Mengele.' That one sentence goes on ringing with the note, a wolf-note perhaps, of contradiction at the heart.

Schumann's *Kinderszenen*, with its *Foreign Lands and Places*, *Blind Man's Bluff*, *At the Fireside* and *Dreaming*—this last being what she played, to order, to her one-man audience taking time out to dream—brings to that particular music room the deep, irresolvable counter-shock of history. Between Schumann's child's-play and reality's facts lies the impossible lesson, about ourselves, our history, our capabilities, for which a lifetime's learning is not enough.

9—Classified

If the convent taught me how to save my soul and fail the eleven plus—the nuns disapproved of it and refused to teach to it—the years that followed, after the family moved from Edinburgh to Oxford, taught me to forget my soul and pass exams. Most of the nuns taught well, with passion and intelligence. But their aims were otherworldly. At the Oxford High School lessons were streamlined towards an altogether lesser destination: Oxbridge entrance. The year of transition was difficult for me as, aged fourteen, I struggled to make sense of a system in which knowledge was a commodity exchanged for use in a public exam. There was no embroidery and no recourse to chapel. Instead, we were constantly graded and classed, our places set on a moveable sliding-scale of test results. We shifted up or down, beta plus, alpha minus, in the league tables of an education which was without mystification, and without mystery.

At eleven, with my small history of failing exams, I would have been refused entry to the High School. At fourteen, I was given the second chance refused to many. Gradually, I learned to manage the new rules, making my way from bottom to top set, from shy incompetent to what was then called, as if we were pieces of uncut cloth, Oxbridge material. If, however, I never quite bought into the kind of obedience required—obedience which was not the inherently impossible, lifelong reversal of 'that first disobedience', but the game-playing obedience of winning competitions—I was also grateful for the tough, secular perspective the High School gave me. It was liberal, agnostic and, in the late sixties, fairly permissive. The inspiring, philosophically-minded headmistress of the time ran the place like an Oxford College, allowing her sixth-formers the freedoms they craved and that were everywhere in the air, so long as they continued to study. At morning assembly she read the Lord's Prayer in the audibly ironic tones of the unbeliever. Perhaps I weathered the spirit of the age—full of freedoms but, for women, without safeguards—precisely because those two institutions, in their different ways, set their gods above personal fads, fashions and inclinations.

Nevertheless, throughout those years of public examinations— years which had their intellectual rewards and led, for me, in the appointed direction—I kept hold of something, a kind of mental talisman, that would remain ungradable and unclassifiable, that would resist the metrics of success by which I was judged and would come to judge, and which cut across the straight and narrow routes of academic ambition. Call it a cross stitch.

But it had another name, too. Between school and university I gave it a chance, and spent nine months in London at the Royal College of Music, studying cello. But that road never opened for me. I was temperamentally unsuited to solo performance, bored by practising and not good enough to do without, and at the end of it I went to Oxford to do English, as planned. So music, that other language whose roots lay deep in my life, went underground and stayed there for nearly thirty years. When it was ready to emerge, it was in another form. It taught me, however, something of the musician's ways: that listening is the activity which lies deep in all the arts of sound—an activity which sometimes leads to other conversations, free and uncharted, beyond what we know, but capable all the same of piercing to the bone.

10—Last Call

Bats! The air is full of them, flittering rags, scraps of shadow. They're there and not there, seen and gone in the flick of an eyelid. They tease my ears with their thin high squeaks, not exactly notes that you could pitch on a scale, but tiny smudges, soft rubbings of air. They diphthong into quiet everywhere, like tiny leathers on an invisible windscreen. I'm told you stop hearing bats when you're older. I shall miss them. Even now I wonder how many of their short pips slip my ears, gone from my hearing, leaving a quiet that's only so many missed notes. I sit here in the evenings in front of the open shutters, all ears.

I saw one once. It was sitting on a man's hand, injured, its wings folded like a broken umbrella, its tiny dog face passive with terror. I remember wondering what on earth it was. Then he stretched out the wing, a wide cobwebby tent of veins, scalloped and rigged with raw thin rods. It was so much bigger than the little bat body, it made me think of those rickety, old-fashioned aeroplanes. I never saw a bat so close again.

Nights are the best time here. I sit up late at the open window, collating my notes from the day's researches. Outside seems even hotter than indoors—its stuffy closed attic all lumbered with stars. The day's used heat beats up from the tiles below. Opposite's a blank wall, blank as a page. A small back terrace, hung with the hair of some withered tomato plants, is the one thing that breaks the monotonous plaster. The owners must be away. Above I can trace a skyline of aerials, square meshed faces standing on stick legs. They look like thin crowds, straining to catch the news. Tonight, a quarter moon tangles in them low down, like a dead fish in a net. I can hear the chatter of televisions all round, and behind it the chronic ground bass of cars.

August in Rome—a crazy time to come, I know! But at least it's quiet, everyone away, and the churches open, empty and cool. So I go happily poking about on my own, peering into all the darkest side-chapels, rummaging behind altars, exploring the mustiest of crypts. I have a plan to write a book about relics, religious and literary. Eye of newt, toe of frog. Never mind Michaelangelo, Bernini and the rest, give me a dim altar grating and a moth-eaten saint with black claw hands and leathery features, and I'm happy as a sandboy. Mostly they have a sad, apologetic look, of being not quite as incorruptible as they should be. Finger bones peep out, eye sockets have been stuffed with cotton wool, feet poke through worn shoes, poor things. There they are, sidelined by time, put away from view, no longer admired and touched and prayed to. No-one except me comes peering, half on my knees, to see how they go, these bizarre, forgotten sleeping beauties, dressed and half-fleshed for the last call. It must seem, to them, to be taking an eternity. The best are the Capuchins, as I guessed they would be. What a joke! Thousands of monks, disjointed and hung in patterns on the walls: the chapel of skulls, the chapel of thigh bones, the chapel of shoulder blades. All sizes of bone are leased, till the Last Day, to this cheerful frippery. Vertebrae, I learn, make the prettiest bone chains, ribs the best curves. The coccyx is an intricate piece of open work, excellent for lanterns. To think that, at the last day, all these festoons and tendrils will come unstuck from the walls, and rattle together again to peg up the old flesh. What a come-down, I think, as I wander among them. This is not marrow-shaking horror, but pure wit—a fantastical usefulness and gaiety of purpose.

On my way out I couldn't help but observe the elderly friar who stood at the exit, pointing a finger-of-death at a bag marked *Offerte*. 'One more for the unfinished arch, Brother? For that chink in the lantern? An arm or a leg, Sister, for art, for art! Look, one more scapula, a clavicle for the chapel!' (*Can these bones live?* Not too soon, one hopes, after all that work.)

Relics, I meditate, are everywhere in this country: Tasso's hair, Galileo's finger, Shelley's heart—beloved body, to have and to hold, if only in parts. Even the hem of a garment will do; something to touch, literally, the imagination. To pay and to see. It's the tourist trade, too, of course—though these, forgotten in dusty chapels, are of no interest to anyone.

Last night I was sitting at my desk as usual. It was about eleven thirty. I was just thinking of going to bed when the telephone rang, making me jump for my life. For a second I stared at it, sitting puggish at my elbow. Then quickly, before the next ring could jigger my nerves again, I lifted the receiver. Immediately, as if it had waited long enough for an answer, a woman's voice asked: 'Luciana?'

'No,' I answered, both relieved and a little disappointed. 'There's no Luciana,' I explained. 'It must be the wrong number.' To my surprise the voice insisted.

'Luciana?' she asked suspiciously.

'Sorry, there's no Luciana,' I repeated. 'What number did you want?' There was a longish pause. Then the voice turned querulous: 'Luciana? What is the matter?'

I was nonplussed. Evidently Luciana sounded rather unlike herself, but not enough to make a difference. I almost put the phone

Life from Sixteen Angles

down. But something hurt and urgent about the voice stopped me. Anyway, I needed to clear this up and be sure she didn't call again. So, slowly and patiently, as if speaking to a foreigner, I asked:

'What number did you ring?'

'The number?' She sounded flummoxed. 'The number is here somewhere.' I heard the sound of papers being shuffled. 'Somewhere, I cannot see. It is here.' I tried another tack:

'Who are you?'

'It's Vittoria!' she exclaimed. 'Don't you recognise me?' I almost laughed. 'Listen Luciana,' she hurried on, impatient of my games and prevarications, 'the time has come. I have to warn you.'

'What about?' The question slipped out before I could stop it.

The pause was so long that I thought she must be suspecting the mistake. I stared out of the window. I could hear the small aerial pips of the bats in the shadows outside—tiny, high disturbances of the quiet, almost the other side of sound. They flitted across the funnel of the courtyard, fidgety and fast between shadow and sight. As I watched I remembered something I had once learned. Bats fly by sound. So these were bouncing their notes off the stone walls, the shutters, the pantiles, and then, I thought, also off the softer different shape that I made, sitting at the open window. I tried to imagine myself in their ears, as their radar voices hit the obstacles of the world to clear a passage through them. They were sounding me out, deciphering the sound of my shape in the lamp-light, translating my looming head and shoulders into notes—bat notes, scored in their tiny brains. And if they heard the forms of things like that, they must hear nothing too, I thought, all sorts of nothing, in varied bulks and densities, nothing, thick and thin. They must dial through it with their queer high pips, sensing its absences. Pipistrelles, I remembered. What a crude, deaf instrument I was by comparison.

'It's the end!' The voice suddenly thrilled into my ear, quivering with pent-up emotion. I had almost forgotten her, my intrusive late-night caller, interrupting the delicate fabrications of the dark. Wearily, I applied my ear again to the receiver.

'But I don't know you,' I warned. Then my curiosity got the better of me: 'What's the matter?'

'Luciana.' The voice was peremptory now, as if no longer to be deflected by fanciful impersonations. 'It's the end, I tell you. They know it also. It's what I always said. You remember how I warned you?'

'I am very sorry ...' I apologised.

'But no!' she exclaimed. 'It is what we all expect. All the signs are there.' Here she lowered her voice to a conspiratorial contralto.

'You have only to watch the birds. Have you noticed the birds, the way they flock together in shifting shapes above the city? Most people don't notice the birds. It is a sign.' I was baffled. Then suddenly she seemed to light on the explanation. 'The world will end in a year's time. Like that. Poof! You see? It is true. I have also read it in a scientific paper.'

'What a pity', I proposed.

'A pity?' she echoed, genuinely perplexed. Then agreed. 'Yes, I have had such an unhappy life, Luciana. I am ninety-five, you remember. Ninety-five.' I wondered if it was appropriate to compliment her on the fact. But her longevity seemed part of the general threat. How could I inform her it was all based on a mistaken number? I waited. This was ridiculous. It was nearly midnight and I wanted to go to bed. But Vittoria was suddenly struck by a new suspicion:

'Luciana, you are deceiving me. I can tell.'

'Not at all', I explained helplessly.

'Always', she interrupted. 'Always you have deceived me, ever since I can remember. I know you. But soon nothing will matter anymore, I tell you.' She waxed almost lyrical at the thought: 'Soon it will be over, all over. Do you know how old I am?'

'Ninety-five, I think.'

'*Exactly!*' She was triumphant with calculations.

Meanwhile, the bats flickered in the corner of my eye. Perhaps, after all, it was better not to hear every note. There would be so much noise out there, beyond the muffling vacuum of space: there would be the roar of the sun, the crackle of a last star. I looked up. One of them, on cue, skidded and flashed forever out of existence. The moon curled round, a clear bright comma to nothing. What a racket of catastrophes up there would fill our ears if we could only hear it. And the moon too, I thought—what was the sound of that empty white mass turning endlessly through space? What was the sound of something turning on nothing?

It was eerily quiet outside. The moon had moved up out of the way of the aerials. They stayed like a scribble on the dark, a thin, scrawny italic on the skyline. The silence batted strangely against my ears.

I decided to take the initiative. 'I must go now', I asserted, trying to be firm, my voice wavering, to my mind, between Luciana's and my own. The proposal seemed to wake my caller from a trance.

'Go?' she snapped. 'Where will you go? It is too late, I tell you. Much too late.' I looked wearily at my watch. 'In a year,' she continued, 'just a year, it will be over. We know it now for sure. Even the . . .'

I could hear the open, expectant hum of the line that went from my ear to her mouth, my mouth to her ear, the chance fact of our communication across the night. She had called, and found me. But I was not Luciana. I was tired. It was after midnight and I wanted to sleep. I didn't want to hear how terrible Vittoria's life had been. I didn't want to know how all the world's problems might be solved by a final arithmetical solution. I wanted to hear the quiet, and fall asleep in it, alone.

Cautiously, I removed the receiver from my ear. I could hear the voice running on and on, calculating its disillusionment in round figures, trumpeting its despair with numerical passion. With luck, I decided, she wouldn't remember this particular wrong number. I held my breath . . .

and slowly, lowered the phone into its cradle. The quiet received it with a tiny click.

11—Sotto Voce

It was the quiet I remember. Somehow, quiet was always a presence in the house, necessary for the work that went on there. As children, we were shooed out of the way when Kenneth was at work—the television turned down, records played softly, friends hosted in our separate rooms behind shut doors. *The telephone is an instrument of the devil*, he would rage, especially on returning from the pub in the evening when all grievances were let loose, usually in the form of some universal excoriation. The fault was large and abstract, civilisation itself, or the absence of it. Whatever slight or hurt or anxiety he suffered, it was always displaced onto wild generalisation, or diffused into the alcohol which was his daily solace and would prove his end. Personal feelings were not of interest, so that, in a sense, we never really knew him, or never knew the origins of the passions we sometimes witnessed.

He was probably a rather lonely man, whose life of composition never quite fitted the professional, then professorial, role he filled in the university. If the times had been different, he might have been happier as a freelance composer, and my mother happier as a working wife. But fifties fatherhood, like fifties motherhood, was a rigid divider, and the idea of admitting to his working-class parents that he had no job and that his wife went out to work, was simply out of the question. So after a year in Rome studying composition with Petrassi, he knuckled under: taught the Royal Marines at Deal, accepted a Gregory Fellowship at Leeds, then moved to a lectureship in composition at Edinburgh University. With the exception of two years in Oxford, Edinburgh gave him a lifelong home, if always an adopted one—one in which he never quite figured as a Scottish composer. Nationalities, those accidental facts of time and place, are born, and die with us.

Yet it was Scotland, particularly the Western Highlands, that Kenneth loved, and to which he escaped for holidays and sabbaticals as soon as the family could afford a car. First in rented caravans, then in cottages, my brother and I, sometimes together, sometimes alone, occasionally with friends, accompanied him on those trips to Arran, Mull, Skye, to Torridon or Ardnamurchan. My mother increasingly stayed at home.

Those escapades north, which continued into our late twenties, were intimate yet impersonal, companionable yet silent. We worked or read, walked the dog, cooked our own simple meals, and sat in the pub of an evening, when Kenneth would puff on his pipe and an easy trickle of chat would pass between us. Those silences were effortless and relaxed, as if in that atmosphere something were being attended to which mattered. At any rate, we lived with a kind of untroubled inwardness, contentedly, our eyes full of the scenery around us and our ears stretched, in a sense, by the spaciousness of its quiet. At some level that assumption of silence became second nature. It taught us to think, whatever that means: to daydream, meditate, wonder, consider, cogitate, peruse. It might have been dull, but it wasn't, and year after year, into our late twenties, my brother and I returned for those free holidays. Kenneth, I think, was glad of the company.

Looking back, it was as if we were excavating a space around ourselves—a space by which life itself could be thrown into relief. We were fair-weather walkers, not ambitious for any heights, happiest on the shorelines and along the glens, noting the weather or the birds, but mostly, perhaps, registering the deep indifference of those things and letting it permeate. The strange consolation of nature's quiet is that it does not console at all, but makes consolation irrelevant. That was a lesson we carried with us for life. There are few stories to tell about those weeks because, though we talked and walked together, and sat of an evening over a pint in the local bar, discussing new compositions, new writings, they were really a kind of self-absenting time—a way of putting self to one side, which is the same as saying, going so far within oneself that there's almost nothing there.

⚹

It was in the summer of 1973, while we were staying in Portree on the Isle of Skye, that news of Nanny's death arrived. It was hardly unexpected, and it should have been a relief. For she had been in Stanley Royd, the old Wakefield asylum, for some years after evidence of increasing dementia made it hard for her husband, Tom, to look after her at home. It was a sad fate—made more poignant by the fact that Tom himself had worked for much of his life as an 'attendant', that is, porter-cum-orderly-cum-nurse, in that same asylum. He knew at first hand its regime—once enlightened, even pioneering but, particularly in its later years, overcrowded and understaffed. Opened in 1818 as the West Riding Pauper Lunatic Asylum, by the late twentieth century, like many others of its type, it had outgrown its use, and was closed in 1995. Tom, a kindly but reticent man, who sang in the local church choir and also played the piano by ear, but whose general education was scant, never spoke about his work there. It seems likely, however, that he took part in the many musical events, pantomimes, dances and theatrical performances which were held in the purpose-built theatre. Male attendants, who worked in the men's wards, needed no previous experience, but were usually employed for their extra gifts: because they could 'read music, play a musical instrument or possessed a good singing voice'. An advertisement for an asylum shoemaker in 1898, for instance, stipulated an ability 'to play either the cello or the violin' to help out with the orchestra. Tom, who probably joined in the 1920s after the war, might well have been called upon to play the piano—there were about a dozen scattered in various wards—for the 'ward concerts', those welcome, impromptu sing-alongs recalled by patients and staff alike. The vast Georgian building, designed on the panopticon model which allowed for observation of wards from a single vantage point, was, by the middle of the twentieth century, a frightening, confusing insti-tution, full of patients with very different mental problems, and some, perhaps, with none at all, who had merely been unlucky, workless, depressed, or who had effectively grown up in the place, as single mothers or the children of single mothers. The hospital functioned as restraining gaol, as well as workhouse, poorhouse, refuge or respite home for the otherwise unplaceable.

Tom's silence about Stanley Royd, whether from necessary confi-dentiality or inherited taboo, was matched by a similar silence about his time in the trenches during the First World War. Only on his death bed did I find him, once, to my amazement, half-raving about the Tommies, the duckboards, the blood and the mud of it. Of his work at Stanley Royd, where he probably also minded and nursed returning shell-shocked soldiers—in 1920 there were about 122 of them there—he remained resolutely silent. His own shocks of war, like other shocks he may have encountered, or administered, at the asylum, were buried deep in a silence that only the morphine of his last weeks helped to break. In the end, with a kind of cruel irony, as if its shadow could never be escaped, Stanley Royd took into its grim embrace, for the last sad years of her life, the woman Tom loved.

Nanny's symptoms had begun to show some years earlier. I remember sudden pauses in the middle of the simplest actions; wandering, halting sentences which broke into tearfulness; the ten-dency to fold and unfold a piece of paper, like an unsent letter; the slowly tapping fingers as if, words escaping her, she were searching for something, or remembering the rhythm of a once playable tune. I own a tablecloth made by her in those later years. It is beautifully embroidered in feather stitch, with elaborate green leaves and blue flowers at each corner—except for the fourth where something goes amiss, and a single flower, half blue, half red, bulges unnaturally out of all proportion. It reads like the script of a break-out, an unruly caper, a loud cry for help.

That evening, when he heard the news of her death, Kenneth was distraught. We had never seen him cry before, but that evening the tears rolled down his cheeks from some ancient source, unstoppable and unappeasable. We sat with him all evening in the public bar of a hotel while he wept silently, occasionally disguising a sob, gazing at something far away on the table in front of him. Nothing could enter that grief, and nothing could console it. It went far back—perhaps to those childhood trips between different worlds: down the brick ginnel at the back of the house to sing at the cathedral, to the grammar school, then to Oxford on a Classics scholarship; but above all to the memory of those hands that had played the piano to him in the very beginning: the *Hokey Cokey* or *Old King Cole*—hands which spent their last years desperately fidgeting for expression in the crowded halls of Stanley Royd.

All we could do that evening was to go on chatting around him, keeping up a semblance of normality, while the quiet that was his natural atmosphere wrapped him round, removing him to a world we could not enter.

It became, of course, another of those deep silences from which, in time, the sounds of a new composition would emerge. All the agony, the memory, the guilt, would eventually burst through their barriers in the extraordinary hour-long music of the second symphony, the 'Sinfonia Mistica', with its *sotto voce* dedication, 'In Memoriam F. L.'—to his mother, Florrie Leighton.

12—Gowks and Lappies

Old Bert walked me down the hill. It was a warm August day and the moors were topped with purple. I'd bought some peppers at the village shop at which he glanced in disdain, commenting: 'What's them, then?' Bert had lived in the valley ever since he was a boy. He remembered scavenging for coals from the spills of the coal trucks when the iron mines were still open, and he remembered the general strike of 1926 which turned out to be the mines' conclusive deathblow. After that, the story of the valley was of one long economic decline and depopulation, or, seen the other way, of one steady return to its natural state. But Bert stayed in the place, living in the same small terraced cottage, updale from Rosedale, and never travelling more than ten miles beyond it. He knew every inch of the land around him, but the world beyond was foreign territory. He knew where to find the biggest bilberries, in places that were 'blae o'er', before the sheep got to them. He knew where there were sloes, where the best young nettles could be picked. He knew the ways and names of every bird and plant, though they were not necessarily the names we knew. He owned a few hens which he housed in a rickety coop on the verge of our one-track road, and he was a good shot at the rabbits and pheasants which then hung, bloodily, in his larder.

Bert would lend a helping hand at the local farms when needed. He knew a wether-lamb from a gimmer-lamb, and in spring I would meet him, often late in the evening, keeping the old farmer company at the door of the lambing shed. Before the days of baby-minders and CT cameras, the farmer would spend half the night, crook in hand, watching and waiting in the March cold. He would stand there silently, quite still, listening to the beasts shift in the straw, watching their moves, patiently awaiting the term of his long year's work. Mostly he stood aside, letting things take their natural course. But if a ewe seemed distressed, or the process took too long, he was in there quick, rooting for the unborn lamb with one hand, checking for a still birth, a breech birth, helping the small creature's exit, in blood and fluid, to the rhythm of the ewe's contractions. Sometimes I would find the two men just chatting quietly, pausing in the watches of the night, sometimes under a fall-out of cold stars, to attend that eventual outcome in the stable of beasts. It was an activity almost as ancient as the race, requiring the same tact, nerve and quietness it had always required. Otherwise, Bert was mostly his own man, living on the land he knew well, never marrying and, when I knew him, probably in his late seventies.

Life from Sixteen Angles

I was on vacation from Hull University, writing a book on women poets—an indoor activity which Bert found incomprehensible. I was never sure he followed much of what I said, and I often struggled to catch his own drift, between the 'yens' and the 'rain-bods', the 'skillies', 'gowks' and 'lappies', the 'pissy-beds' and 'devil's guts'. Bert's world was made up of the birds and plants that returned each year, faithful to a place which, in spite of its short industrial heyday, had not changed much since the prehistoric forests composted into peat. The iron mines on the hillside, where the old railway line once ran, were now protected monuments—rows of crumbling kilns and sidings that looked, my mother declared once in his company, like the Baths of Caracalla. Bert only stared at her with rude incomprehension. For the rest, the rain-bods (curlews) came inland in February as they had always done, their lovely curling calls like glass flutes heralding rain. The skillies (skylarks) improvised endlessly on a theme of Vaughan Williams on the hillside, the lappies (lapwings) tumbled in noisy falling displays, day and night, while the gowks (cuckoos), one or two at most, took up their posts each year in late April, the spring trials of their calling minor thirds eventually resolving into summer's major.

As we walked back that day Bert asked me where I worked, and I tried to explain a bit about teaching and students—things that depended on an activity I doubt he had much use for: writing. At one point he lapsed into silence, pondering perhaps a life so different from his own. And then, looking sideways, as if at something far away in the hills, he said very quietly: 'Will ye lie wit' me, then?' I thought I'd misheard, and stumblingly replied: 'Eh, sorry?' But he only said it again, more softly this time, and further away: 'Will ye lie wit' me?' It was touching, ancient, wistful, a phrase from some long-gone impossible pastoral, almost bookish, if it weren't also so matter of fact. It was the question of a man who perhaps had not had occasion to ask before, or who took his cues from the natural world around him. For myself, all I could do was pretend I hadn't heard or hadn't understood. I changed the subject, and chattered instead about this and that: the weather, how long it would last, and then, with an old instinct for safety, about my mother who was coming to visit at the weekend.

I don't think Bert held it against me. He continued to bring us eggs from time to time, or to drop by for a whisky. He'd let us know when the rain-bods were boding rain, or the gowk was back in the valley in April, or the devil's guts were making havoc with our small garden. He never translated his local idioms; we just learned to translate them for ourselves. But some weeks later, in the middle of another conversation across the garden wall, I did catch him, as he turned from me, suddenly muttering in all innocence to himself—as if he'd been working on it slowly and now realised where the problem lay: 'Well it coomes to summat when we have Eyeties teaching English in our universities!' It was a fair summary, I thought, even if not exactly the reason for our difficulties of communication.

13—A Place

That summer I was in Rome again, working on translations of
Italian poetry. One morning my landlady, who lived in the flat four
floors below and must have been waiting, caught me on the stairs.
That stairwell could whip up the merest whisper into echoes, so
that, from below, she would probably have heard my door shutting.
No doubt she also knew that I always used the stairs. The lift, with
its creaking winch and nervous shudders, filled me with horror. The
first time I used it, packed with my suitcases, it groaned angrily all
the way up, and then stopped, pointedly, a step short of the fifth
floor. The stairwell, which wound round the open lift cage, was lit
by cracked, frosted-glass windows which threw puzzles of sunshine
on the floor. At night I had to race the time switch, which invariably
left me, somewhere between the fourth and fifth floors, stranded
in the dark.

   That morning la Signora, as I always called her, was standing at
her door as I passed. She raised a hand in salutation and beckoned
me to her side. A handsome woman, with dark brown eyes and fine
white hair drawn back in a bun, she spoke an old-fashioned, cour-
teous Italian and invariably used the polite form of 'lei'. She laid
a hand on my arm. She would be very pleased, she informed me,
if I would care to dine with them that evening. I thanked her and
she smiled, tapping me once on the arm. 'At seven', she added, and
nodded approvingly.

   At seven precisely, then, and a little apprehensively, I rang the
bell. I waited a few moments but there was no sound. I was just
about to ring again when I heard feet shuffling towards the door. I
stood back. There was a long pause, a queer mesmerising silence,
which made me wonder if I'd imagined the feet—or was someone
really standing, listening, on the other side? I checked that I was
on the right floor. Yes, the first. As the seconds ticked on, the sense
of someone lying in wait became unbearable. I coughed and rus-
tled the bunch of roses I had bought. They were rather cheap and
I glanced at them in embarrassment. Then, just as I was raising a
hand to ring again, I noticed in the middle of the door a tiny round
peephole. So I was right. Behind that globular lens, impenetra-
ble as a bull's-eye, was another human eye coolly observing me. I
stared blindly back into the glass, then slowly, without thinking,
edged nearer as if, that way, I might see into its distorting convex
darkness. Suddenly, from the other side, a peremptory childish
voice called out: 'Chi è?' This stopped me in my tracks. Fixing the
rude cyclops with a stare, I explained rather clumsily that I was
the tenant from upstairs. The voice translated my answer into

a simple: 'Mammà. It's her.' 'Well, why don't you open!' Almost immediately there was a tremendous racket of bolts being drawn, a chain being removed and a key being turned. The door opened creakily on its hinges.

In the dim light, a small hunched woman with a drawn white face stared up at me, then stepped back to let me in. She muttered something I couldn't understand. 'It's her', she called out over her shoulder once again. Having been thus identified, I was ushered in. To my relief la Signora immediately appeared in a doorway. She came quickly forward and led me to the sitting room. 'Come in, come in. This is Laura, my daughter', she explained. Laura herself had scuttled away into a back room. I held out my bunch of red roses, one of which, I noticed, had already lost its head. But she accepted it with delight and left me for a while to find a vase.

A round table hung with a white damask tablecloth was laid for four in a corner of the room. On the walls were some old portraits in oils, one of a severe looking man in spectacles and military uniform, another of a young boy sitting on the side of a well in a garden, another of a pretty girl standing by her bicycle. The portraits brought an odd sense of space into the small room, where two punishingly upright chairs flanked a low coffee table. The only other piece of furniture was a glass cabinet full of fans and blue china. The shutters opened onto a dreary cylindrical courtyard, where a panopticon of windows looked in from all sides. I realised how lucky I was to have a view from my upper flat, if only of walls, aerials and sky. Such eye-space is precious in Rome, where most people live like prisoners between high walls. In the courtyard, a mournful stunted palm straggled up against the opposite wall, its blades fingering any breeze that might come.

La Signora returned with her flowers in a vase and bade me sit down. Slowly she lowered herself onto the chair beside me. 'The heart,' she explained, with a deprecating flutter of her hand, as if to mimic its actions. 'It feels its age.' I reached for one of those easy, sinuous Italian compliments which cannot be translated into English except in clichés. I noticed how a certain beauty hung about her still, an indefinably conscious grace, though she must have been well into her eighties. She was wearing a plain black dress, relieved by a green brooch: a finely sculptured Medusa's head with a straight Greek nose and hair flaming into exquisite carved snakes. She caught my look and explained: 'It is made of lava, from Vesuvius. It is soft stone and easy to work. This', she paused, 'was given to me many years ago ...' She smiled one of those distantly remembering smiles that come readily to the old, then threw in a free challenge: 'By an admirer.'

Life from Sixteen Angles

Suddenly, as if some related thought had crossed her mind, she called out for Laura, her hand visibly agitated on the arm of her chair. Laura appeared at the door: '*Sì, Mammà?*' '*What* are you doing?' Laura glanced at me and shrugged. She was wearing old baggy trousers and a homely checked shirt. Her age seemed indeterminable. She might have been a young girl or an old woman. 'The television', she muttered, tossing her head in its direction. 'But the drinks? Where are the drinks?' When she spoke to Laura there was a fierceness in la Signora's voice which took me by surprise. '*Sì Mammà*', she answered in a curious little clockwork voice, and shuffled away. La Signora turned back to me. 'Laura', she raised her eyebrows, 'is married to the television. It is impossible to drag her away. I sometimes say it is so bad for her. But then, poor thing, it is her life.'

It was on the tip of my tongue to ask more, but she had already changed the subject. 'Now, tell me about yourself. You are studying?' I explained about my work of translation, about the difficulties of turning Italian verse, with its easily inverted syntax and innumerable rhymes, into English. Somehow, in spite of myself, I told her all kinds of other things too. Her eager questions teased them out of me. '*Che brava!*' she repeated, as I warmed to her interest, as well as to the clinking glass of Martini which Laura had brought on a tray and which seemed to congratulate me, volubly, on all my plans. La Signora agreed, praised, approved, with an attention I found quietly seductive. I had some sympathy with that admirer. As I slipped from one thing to another, I occasionally wondered when the other guest would arrive. In the backroom I could hear the witter of the television, turning out endless stories of its own. I thought the two of them must lead a pretty dull life, shut in this small flat with only their own company. The idea seemed to justify my unusual garrulousness.

At last, after I seemed to have spilled out half my life, Laura appeared with a tureen of spaghetti and I was hurried to the table. No-one mentioned the other guest and I didn't like to ask. So I sat where I was shown, with the expectant empty place on my left. La Signora stumbled slightly as she lowered herself into her chair. I reached out to help, but she waved me away. At that moment, however, she noticed that something was missing and turned in reproach to her daughter: 'But the salt?' Laura hurried dutifully back to the kitchen. The absence of the salt seemed a deadly serious matter. La Signora then returned to her soft tones and explained, almost mystically: 'I have always had a weak heart. All my life.' She tapped it, encouragingly. I offered my commiserations, but she refused them like an unwanted gift. 'No, no,' she

insisted, 'you should see me sometimes. I am quite breathless.'
Here she held her breath and put her hand on the place where the
thing should be beating. She might have been about to sing an
aria of love. Laura, who had returned with the salt, suddenly inter-
jected passionately: 'At night! It is terrible, sometimes, at night.'
She shook her head hopelessly and stared at the tablecloth.

This was the first time I had had a chance to look at her. Her
gaunt face was white as a ghost's, made whiter by the shock of
black hair that hung on either side. It was a child's face, burdened
with an adult expression. The lines around her mouth were pulled
down to one side, like a tragic mask fixed in distress. Her eyes,
however, were small and slanted. Between her mischievous eyes
and the puckered lines of her jaw, she looked as if she was laughing
at herself, at the grim joke life had dealt her. She spoke very little
on the whole, but sometimes words exploded from her, raw and
pungent, as if coming hot from their source. They made a strange
counterpoint to the elaborate, polite courtesies of her mother.
Altogether, it was a bizarre double act to which I, and the empty
place, offered a willing audience.

Now that the table was properly laid, la Signora relaxed. She
started to talk generally about political affairs, the state of Italy
today, the recent elections. The sheer breadth of her knowledge
surprised me, and I was soon out of my depth. She rehearsed Mafia
scandals, the intrigues of businessmen and the corruption of politi-
cians, remembering with nostalgia the days when it was safe to walk
the streets and the trains ran on time. I nodded warily. At one point
Laura suddenly cried out, as if she could contain it no longer: 'I tell
them so!' At this la Signora lost her temper. 'Don't talk nonsense,'
she raged, her hand trembling on the edge of the table like a tem-
perature gauge. Then, apologetically, she reminded me not to go out
at night, there were so many delinquents about, pickpockets and
drug addicts, and those strange men, you know, on the Lungotevere,
who wore women's clothes. She had read all about it in the papers.
She had also heard recently of a friend who had been dragged
halfway down the street by thieves on a motorbike. 'They even steal
from nuns', she whispered in a lowered voice. 'Nothing is sacred.'

This seemed to trigger something in Laura's imagination, for
she added jerkily, gazing into the middle distance: 'the nuns are
on fire!' Then she giggled to herself. La Signora stared uncompre-
hendingly, with intense irritation at her daughter. 'But what are you
saying?' she railed. 'It is something she has seen on the television',
she assured me, shaking her head. 'She lives in a world of her own
sometimes.' Then she noticed that my plate was empty. I had eaten
rather fast, without noticing, whether from hunger or nerves.

Life from Sixteen Angles

'Laura, the plate!' she commanded, as if there had been some momentous oversight in leaving me for a few seconds in front of an empty dish. Before I could protest, Laura had rounded up both my own and the unused plate next to me.

The second course arrived on a squealing trolley which, in spite of all Laura's efforts, plunged erratically left then right before approaching the table '*Mamma mia*', she cursed quietly under her breath, while la Signora called out to be careful, to go slowly. She parked it by my elbow, then laboriously transferred the food to the table, refusing any help. This, she seemed to assert, was her role. I noticed that she left a clean plate for the visitor. Either, I decided, it was an idiosyncrasy of her table-laying, or else there was some wayward relative who might turn up at any moment. I lived in hope. Throughout the meal my eye kept returning to that empty plate, set so deliberately and unappetisingly between a knife and a fork. It was like a reproach to the rest of us, a singular mark of abstinence. 'Have some more', la Signora insisted at each course. 'Just a little. Please, it needs finishing. Don't be polite.' The empty plate gaped in hollow mockery of my pile: veal, courgettes, salad, then a cornucopia of fruit. The absent visitor was kept up to date in clean plates.

In fact, no-one ate very much except myself. Laura gulped down her allotted portions, then stared in boredom at the tablecloth like a child waiting to be dismissed. La Signora always had something on her plate, but it was the same morsel, I noticed, retained for politeness' sake, to keep me company. 'You must eat,' she declared at one point, tapping me encouragingly on the arm. 'Laura and I, we need very little. But you...' Then she stopped, as if seeing something very far away, where the open question went on calling for an answer. 'But you have your work to finish, and you are young', she concluded.

I was glad to leave the table when we finished. Laura was ordered to make coffee and went off into the kitchen, pushing the crazy loaded trolley in front of her. La Signora took my arm and we returned to our two hard chairs. 'Now I will show you some photographs,' she said, drawing out an album from under the coffee table and bringing her chair near to mine. 'Laura!' she called out, in one of those passionate nonsequiturs I was becoming used to. 'Remember! with milk.' '*Sì, mammà.*' 'Laura', she informed me, 'does everything in the house. She cleans, cooks, washes up. She has learned over the years. When I was young, we had servants to do all that. Now, it is different.' She sighed, then added: 'I don't know how I would manage without her.' 'She is magnificent', I declared, suddenly meaning it. 'Does she ever go out?' 'Almost never', la Signora snapped. The tone was almost triumphant. Then it modified into sadness: 'Poor girl. But it's impossible. She cannot go on her own. You see how she is. It would be too dangerous, and I am too old.'

Suddenly Laura, who had returned to the room, interrupted, declaring with a look of forlorn amazement: 'I went out once.' She stared at the memory of that outing which seemed to hang somewhere between the table and the wall. 'Where did you go?' I asked, realising this was the first time I had addressed her all evening. But having had her say, she clammed up. 'Don't take any notice of her', la Signora pronounced. 'Laura, don't be foolish. Go and make the coffee.' I felt I had just caught a tiny thread of some other story, some other place, elusive as a narrowing path. But la Signora drew me back. 'Look,' she invited, putting the album on her knee and opening it at the first page, 'this is my family.'

The first thing I saw was Laura, the fourth of five children, four girls and a boy, ranged along a wall in sailor suits, her dark pigtails sticking out at an angle under her hat. She was unmistakeable, with her slanting eyes and surprised hair. La Signora herself then appeared in a hazy studio profile, her brown hair tied softly back in a bun, dreamily beautiful as I suspected she would be—a woman with admirers! Slowly, as the pages turned, I tracked them through the years: girls on bicycles, in trousers, a boy sitting with an arm round a dog, photographs at the beach, at parties, birthdays, the girls growing up, page by page. Their features slipped into adulthood before my eyes, their looks modifying into something serious, definitive. Yet beside her tall, brown-eyed sisters, Laura looked always small and different, pale and clownish. There was a picture of her as a young woman, grinning at the camera in a tartan skirt and beret, holding one of her sister's babies in her arms. For some reason, on the same page, there was a loose photo that seemed to have lost its place. It showed a troupe of girls in gymslips doing exercises, their arms windmilling round them. La Signora explained: 'It was the fashion then, in schools. Mussolini, you know . . . he made them all do physical exercises, every day. It was ... healthy.' After a pause she added: 'Laura did them at home, sometimes. She didn't go to school, of course. Papa thought it might help.' Laura, who had returned with the coffee, set up a wail of recognition. *'Mamma mia!'* she reminisced in horror. 'Up and down, up and down.' And for a moment I imagined her, the hunched shoulders and awkward, uncoordinated body in training for her country, practising to be a strong mother for the Motherland. I shivered for a moment at the thought of that history ... and of other Lauras, in less lucky places.

It was a relief to turn over the page and leave the photo casually tucked in, out of order. There was Laura again, as a young girl, standing next to a boy with his arm round her shoulders. 'My two youngest', la Signora pointed out, and then stopped. 'Your son?' I asked. There was a long pause. From the silence I half guessed what was coming, and bit my tongue. 'He is dead', she asserted. 'He was very young. There was nothing we could do. My Carlo.' 'Dead', Laura repeated, as if she were still learning new words and trying to attach them to the world she knew. 'I am so sorry.' But la Signora intervened to help me out of my difficulty. 'And these are my other children and grandchildren.' The last pages of the album were full of them, snapped into life and then hustled through the years: babies, toddlers, schoolchildren. It was like watching life in fast motion, the face changing every second, subtly remodelled by the quiet engineering of the years. Photographs have always made me sad. They snatch at moments, turning life into a desert of smiling attitudes, poses for posterity, with everything else hidden out of sight. There were no more photographs of Carlo after that one, and Laura, I noticed, gradually started to develop the lines of pain she showed today, though she went on smiling.

I was glad when the pages came to an end and I was freed from the burden of all those lives. 'Another coffee?' la Signora offered. My attention swung back with relief to the present. I looked at my watch. 'Just one, thank you. Then I must go.' 'But before you go,' she quietly proposed, pouring the coffee into my tiny china cup, 'I wonder if you would play a game of draughts?' 'With pleasure', I responded. 'With Laura', she explained. 'I used to play with her often in the past, but now, you see, my hands tremble too much. I knock the pieces off the board. I know she would be so pleased.' 'I would enjoy it', I affirmed with genuine feeling. It would be a relief not to listen or talk for a while.

Laura, on cue, was already standing in the doorway with a wooden box under her arm. '*Ecco!*' she announced, and brought it to the table. La Signora vacated her chair, gesturing to me that she would be in the other room. Laura started laying out the pieces. So this is what she'd been waiting for, I thought. This was her game. 'Black or white?' she rattled when it was ready. I chose white.

'When did you last play?' I asked. She made a wave-like motion with her hand, to show how far in the past it was: 'Many many years.' 'Did you play when you were little?' I was still haunted by the photographs. But Laura was not going to be lured into words. She tutted and bent her head over the game. 'Black starts,' she declared, her eyes already keyed to the board as if her life depended on it. We made our first simple moves. 'Many years', she repeated a moment later, shaking her shocked hair. Then, staring hard at the board, she smiled, her eyes narrowing almost to nothing as she shut her thoughts behind them.

It was hard to remember that Laura was an old woman. All her attitudes were girlish, as if she had stopped at some point in her teens and was still looking at life from that bashful, apologetic distance of girls who are not sure what they want from it. She was still looking on, in apprehensive distrust of her right to anything, obeying her mother's commands with unwavering conviction. But the one who played draughts was somehow different. At first I played gently, making the obvious moves. But as she started to snap up my pieces I changed tack. I realised she was playing to win, and I couldn't insult her by making it easy. Sometimes, when her concentration flagged, she made a mistake and bit her lip. Sometimes, when she took one of my pieces, she let out a triumphant *'ecco!'* and crossed her arms in satisfaction. All her passivity had gone. She played with the aggressive logic of an invading army. On that black and white board of rigid rules and clear-cut moves she found her place. This language of black and white she could use and understand, unlike that other one which worked by shades and conventions she could not handle. If, in real life, her intelligence was constantly in retreat from some incomprehensible disaster, she found in this grid of simple squares a form with which to prove her power. Here, she could win. In that other language, she was always at a loss.

'You play well', I grumbled, genuinely surprised. Then, as if by some long delayed reaction, she answered my question: 'Carlo, he teach me.' I could think of nothing to say in response, overwhelmed as I was by the small fact she had offered. Of course, I thought. Having said so much, however, she shut her lips, determined nothing else should get past. I asked no more questions.

We were down to our last pieces. At the very end, with a few pieces each, she outwitted me. I was not playing for my life as she was, and I was tired, the evening having taken its toll both of my Italian and my attention. She pounced on my carelessness. 'I win!' she declared as she took my last draught and held it up for me to see. 'I win!' she repeated. *'Bravissima!'* I acknowledged, and looked up at her. The brilliant smile which filled her face made her look, for a moment, like the girl in the photos: the joker, the clown, the one who was different, on her own. Then, as the moment passed and her victory already waned, the dragging jaw of life, pain, loss, reasserted its hold.

As I rose to go at last, I happened to remark to la Signora, for no reason that I could think, 'It was a pity your other guest could not come.' Then I looked round for Laura to say goodbye. But she had already slipped back to her television in the other room. She had no time for courtesies. La Signora was standing very still beside me, lost in thought. Then she took me warmly by the arm, leaning on it quite heavily as we walked to the door. She too was tired, I thought.

I thanked her for the evening and she wished me well in my work, hoping I would dine with them again and, of course, play draughts with Laura who had enjoyed it so. She was especially grateful for that. Then, at the door, as if to lay the ghost of my unease, she suddenly explained quite simply: 'Perhaps he came, and found a place.'

14—Home Again

The gypsy looked at me quizzically that day. A short dark woman with a sallow face, she stood on the doorstep in a green anorak and dark slacks. The minute I opened the door she opened a huge, dark, worn leather bag. 'Hallo pet,' she chanted. 'Would you like something today? Look, I've got dusters, toothbrushes, pegs, needles, whatever you need. Do you need dusters? God bless you. Two for a pound. That's a bargain now. Or a toothbrush? Do you need a toothbrush?' She turned over the small hoard of goods at the bottom of her bag, her voice thrilling with a novelty everything else lacked. I had bought them all before: toothbrushes which exploded bristles in the mouth, needles which snapped at the slightest pressure, dusters which deposited their own small motes of yellow dust everywhere. Yet I never had the heart to send the woman away. She knew it was only a matter of time before I succumbed to some unnecessary purchase—drawn, perhaps, by the music in her voice, the unstoppable lilt of her sweet-talking confidence. This time, however, I must have looked more distracted than usual. There were changes afoot, and I was preoccupied with the business of moving house, in fact moving away from Hull. She stared at me sharply and suddenly changed tack: 'Or a lucky charm, perhaps? Look, for good luck. Blue ones, red ones. God bless you now, pet, I'll give you two for one.'

And I recalled, for a moment, another scene from far back. A child, I was being taken by my Italian grandfather to Naples on the Vesuviana, to visit the museum of San Martino. It was a yearly visit. I never wanted to go, but the adults conspired against my child's reluctance, insisting I should accompany Nonno since I was his only granddaughter. To me it was a wearisome trek, hardly eased by Nonno's patient explanations of Neapolitan history, his recounting of unfamiliar names and dates, alongside his customary inveighings against the church. For me, the only pleasure came at the very end of the visit when, released from history, he left me to myself in the room of the cribs. In those fantastical landscapes, with their mountains, streams, huts and palaces, shepherds and artisans, the miracle in the stable was quickly outclassed, for intricacy and curiosity, by a knife-grinder sharpening knives on a turning wheel, a woman feeding ducks in a pond made of mirrors, by a solitary distant traveller, with a lit lantern, winding his way up a mountain path towards a sky of blue crepe all spangled with stars. In the crib room, I was at home.

Life from Sixteen Angles

So each year I set out with him on the little train, coming into Naples from the south, where the petro-chemicals puffed out stinking fumes and a stench of sulphurous tar came in through the windows. To the right were the grey drums of the gasworks; to the left, the port, cut into square docks and edged with the fanciful skeletons of cranes. Huge grey ships yearned at their moorings. And each year, as we slowed into the station, he issued the same warnings: Naples was dangerous. I was to take his hand, especially in the station. There were many wicked people there and I was to talk to no-one. The danger, I knew, lay beyond the ticket barrier. Inside, there was relative order: the order of those who have something to wait for, somewhere to go, travellers with documents and passports, times and destinations. But beyond the barrier was the unprotected world—a free crazy playground of shoppers, hustlers, gypsies, touts, and the spectacular beggars who roamed its human fields. These last would sidle up, touching my arms sometimes, whining for money, showing off their stumps and squints. 'You must never give money to beggars', Nonno insisted. 'They're charlatans, a load of thieves! Always remember!' Once, I asked if I could give five lire to the little boy with no arms? 'No!' Nonno roared. 'They do it on purpose. It's a scandal. If no-one gave anything, the racket would stop.' How on purpose, I wondered to myself, if he had no arms? But I dared not disobey.

On that day, Nonno's path was suddenly blocked by a florid, black-haired gypsy in a scarlet dress and embroidered black shawl. She struck across his path with a broad smile and an open hand. There was a red carnation in her hair, and bright red matching lipstick on her lips. She tapped him cheerily on the arm, and murmured: 'For the love of God, *Signore*, for the love of God.' In the other hand she held a clutch of holy pictures. But Nonno only scowled and veered past, drawing me with him, gripping my hand harder. 'For the love of God', the woman repeated in surprise, while catching the eye of another man who walked behind us. Then, with a sudden swift gesture, just as I turned to catch a last look, she thrust one of her pictures into my free hand and stroked my hair. '*Bella bambina*', she muttered half absently, and turned back to the man.

At the bus stop Nonno scolded me under his breath: 'I told you not to give money to beggars.' 'But I didn't', I flashed back. 'I didn't give anything.' The picture in my hand was now crumpled and spoiled, though I thought I would keep it, adding it to the ones the nuns gave us on feast days to save in our missals . . . for luck, perhaps. As we climbed into the bus, I cast a glance back at the station where, puzzlingly, among all the wicked people, the charlatans and thieves, a gypsy woman gave away pictures for the love of God.

'How much?' I asked, taking a couple of charms from her hand. 'Five pound', she retorted, too quick to believe. It was ridiculous, I knew, but something in me gave in. I lacked the strength, or perhaps the will, to haggle over luck.

When I looked at the things in my hand, I saw two streaky blue pieces of glass, round and cambered into prisms. They reminded me of teddy bear's eyes. I must have stared at them, lost in thought. 'Lucky charms, pet', the woman assured me, nodding and holding out her hand for the note. I found my purse and drew out a fiver. Was I, perhaps, paying something back, a debt from long ago, or just generally, a debt owed in life? Waking from my daydream, I wished her well and handed over the note.

But she didn't leave instantly. Perhaps she had noticed my inattention, my dreamy distance. Having closed her bag, she paused and, cocking her head to one side, asked a little quizzically: 'Are you going home, then?'

15—Stay

Against the yellow flush of the west, high above the Theatre of
Marcellus, the Portico D'Ottavia with its ancient slab for cutting
fish, above the tall tenements of the Ghetto and its inconspicu-
ous tablet on the wall, commemorating the day in 1943 when the
German SS captured and transported over two thousand Jews—
above all these, in the early autumnal dusk of Rome, flew millions,
perhaps billions of birds. It was as if the sky, one late October day,
had turned to a fresco of shadows; as if the angelic hosts had flown
together in a darkening praise-song, or the mysterious radar echo
of another 'angel' had somehow transposed into echo's own shape,
and left that moving imprint on the sky.

They were flying together in formation, wing to wing, faultlessly, as
if stitched into a single piece of cloth that was being shaken out in
the sky. They were tying and untying gigantic black bows, tunnel-
ling long stockings, swooping through enormous three-dimensional
designs like a flight graph in space. It was a net bagging into the
wind, a point-lace mantilla, a spilling sail. Their invention was
endless. Without leaders or hierarchies, they improvised that mass
choreography in the air, changing tack in a split second, as if a
thought, struck with the inspiration of the moment, showed up in
the neural passages of a vast brain. They made a smokescreen, a
windy shadow, a shifting funnel of ash. That vast, changing, soluble
script wrote and unwrote itself, like a joke against staying, like a
perfectly realised artwork against art.

It was late, and the birds knew it. The day was drawing in, and
the year too. Were they testing the air currents up there, the newly
altering temperatures? Were they feeling the spaces of the sky for
their coming departure? Together, in full view, they dream-traced
their leaving, fantasised their flight-path, and wove a changing
imagination of elsewhere, all the pull and thrill of it, in a flex of
muscle and a sleight of wings.

Wilderness

Once we walked far and wide to find it out,
    beguiled by ways and means,
deer track or eagle span, by cairn or col,
Stac Pollaidh's squinty poll, Blaven's bulk,
some lily-covered lochan under Suilven.

Now, when the sun's long evening light recalls
    sea cemetery walls—
Glen Sannox keeping a handful of you, packed
airtight, where once the wind took the wind
out of you, once we walked side by side—

now, it's anywhere, bewilderingly close to home:
    this roadwork's autopsy,
that waste industrial hoarding foiled by weeds,
or here, in the skin's small houseroom, hive of cells,
there's wilderness enough to be lost in.

Kenneth died too young. Even to his children, fifty eight seemed young and too soon to leave. Moreover, life was just beginning again for him. He was writing new music—compositions infused with a new-found romanticism, passionate but also serene after the turbulent counterpoints of his middle years. He had remarried, was planning to retire early, and had bought a cottage in the Borders to that end. Ironically, too, he had succeeded in giving up alcohol, replacing his nightly pints with lime and soda, and bars of chocolate. But a lifetime of pub-going, coupled with the thing we all thought was safe—his pipe smoking—were, as we learned too late, a slow fuse to throat cancer. By the time it was diagnosed in spring 1988, there were only months to live. During those months he finished what he was composing, put his manuscripts—more than a hundred opus numbers—in order, and maintained a silence about what he was feeling that we children will always remember and, at the time, could only be grateful for.

What was there to say? When the lucky charm runs out, fate can be a dumbfounding companion. Kenneth never burdened us, either with the pain of his dying or with the tiresome minutiae of being ill. He was bored by both of those. What he wanted to talk

Life from Sixteen Angles

about, or rather to hear about, since talking became increasingly difficult, was our own work, our plans and interests. So in those hard months, first in the hospice and finally at home again, I talked to him mostly about poetry: the poets he loved and had set: Patrick Carey, Traherne, Donne, Herbert, Hopkins, in a lifetime of writing for the voice. His was a deeply literary sensibility, as I knew from having helped him find texts for his third symphony— Thomas Browne, Shelley, Barrett Browning—texts that became, in his hands, a touching reflection on what I myself had written. In return, I once bought him a job-lot of pen-nibs, perhaps the last of their kind, from a dingy little shop in the backstreets of Venice, since all his music was written with an old-fashioned dip-pen— one that scratched audibly on the paper, and for which nibs were always in short supply. I now own his copy of my book on *Elizabeth Barrett Browning*, given to him only a couple of years before. There I had written about Aurora Leigh as the disinherited or orphaned daughter who wakes to a world of stones, all gravestones, after the death of her father. The only mark that Kenneth had made, under his name on the title page, was 'page 132 etc'—pointing precisely to those pages about the father's death. Finding it after he died seemed to open a conversation across the stars—a conversation of uncanny premonition on his part, perhaps reproach, perhaps encouragement—which I could then only answer into thin air.

The day before he died, I offered to read some of the psalms out loud. He nodded, and signalled No. 121: 'I will lift up mine eyes unto the hills'—the line he was fond of quoting when we walked together in the Highlands. I read first that one, then went on to another. But suddenly he waved his hand at me to stop. Enough, he croaked. Enough of that. It was a gesture full of the old defiant Kenneth— religious up to a point, as he was, naturally, but then impatient of things pious, churchy. He didn't want prayers; he wanted poetry. So I returned to Hopkins. It was he who constituted our last 'conversation', holding apart our two necessary, nearly unbearable silences— but also, in a sense, holding them together. And the next day, when he was too far away either to see or speak to me, I went on talking and reading to the ear that is, we are told, the very last of our senses to go. It has probably not quite gone from me, yet.

A couple of years later, my brother and I spent Christmas in Brodick on the Isle of Arran. It was mild and often sunny that winter. We watched Goat Fell like a great sundial of each day's shadows; we took trips to Lamlash, with its gentler coastline and island hermitage; we walked in Glen Rosa or up to the Corrie Lochan—names cherished for the haunting they offered us, from years gone by, when we stayed there as students, *en famille*, or when Kenneth had spent a sabbatical there, visited in turn by each of us. And then, towards the end of our stay, we spent an afternoon at Lochranza in the north, where seals basked in the winter sunshine, each on its own rock like a monumental mermaid. They would lollop up out of the water, on fin-hands that looked strait-jacketed, blunt and inept; but once seated, they were streamlined against the blue sky, like sleek sleepy lords of the place, each the king of his own rock-castle.

It was there that we also saw what we had never seen before: a pair of Golden Eagles conducting their extraordinary courtship dance, circling round and round, half together, half apart, with all the controlled insouciance of a long-term flirtation. Suddenly they would break and dive together, meeting talon to talon, one beneath the other, then tumble down like acrobats and fly apart. We lingered, watching those great royal creatures perform their roles of procreation, utterly careless of the little lives below. We stayed spellbound, longer than intended, perhaps because we were also postponing the other reason why we had come.

At the beginning of Arran's most dramatic glen, once mined for its barites—from which barium sulphate derives, used in X-rays of the intestinal tract—is one of those lonely cemeteries, built without chapel or church to guard it from other spirits of the place. It is walled in on all sides, and within hearing of the sea. Glen Sannox looms behind it, glinting in the sunlight or darkening to near-black under louring skies. It can be the most sparkling or the gloomiest of glens. That day, we arrived at about three in the afternoon and the winter light was already dwindling. The hills behind were turning black against the setting sun, and we had to pick our way with care to find the little plot where Kenneth's ashes had been buried.

It seemed lonely there—nothing to hear except small rushes of wind and the whisper of the sea. Was it lonely? Yes, in some ways heartbreakingly so. We felt it like a constriction of breath. Perhaps the living cannot help but imagine how the dead, returning some night, searching for the body's last place, might be stricken to find no-one else around. The small stone, with nothing but a name and two dates, like a terrible reduction to the absurd, seemed to mock our small pilgrimage. So yes, it was lonely, with the sense of absence that such stone markers give when we go hunting for home ground. But of course that loneliness was only ours.

I could think of nothing to leave there but some coloured pebbles, in the Jewish tradition. I gathered them from odd corners of the cemetery and laid them out in a spiral, knowing that a strong wind or perhaps a stray sheep, certainly some smaller creature—rabbit, rat or field mouse, might quickly dislodge them. But it seemed less silly than flowers, in that place which only showed, like evolution itself, the smallness of human things beside the vast, unchanging reality of rocks and hills. I thought, as I constructed my tiny henge of remembrance, that perhaps, after all, it was less lonely than a city cemetery, all cheek by jowl, ash beside ash. Moreover, Kenneth was a solitary man, and this was his chosen landscape for thinking and working. Home ground for being not at home, I thought, as in much of his life—perhaps much of everyone's life? And in the quiet of the dusk, the light slipping away to the other side of the world, inch by inch, we found ourselves, as so often in his company, just listening. A light breeze rustled the nearby grasses, a sheep from the hills let out a long, senseless *baa*, and from the sea-side we could hear a flock of oyster catchers, their restless *peep-peep-peep* coming across the airways in intermittent bursts.

But above all, between those sounds, like the sound of attention in a packed concert hall, we could hear the silence that held them together, giving each one its perfect shape in the approaching night, each note its exact, identifying pitch. It was that silence, after all, which Kenneth had worked in, and worked with, all his life, and which, like a transference of hard listening, he had passed on to others. That evening I carried it away with me. The loneliness was profound and unassuaged, but the sense of attention, like a vast ear shaped by the glacial hollow of the hills, seemed like a last gift from the dead to the living.

In return for it, some four years later, I published the critical book which I dedicated to Kenneth, with its epigraph from a poem he had also set: Barrett Browning's 'A Musical Instrument'. It was a debt I owed—to him, to myself, to the poetry we had shared and the profession I had chosen. But it was not the last word. It took me a few more years, well into my forties, to hear how that silence, the silence of the grave, was calling from me another kind of speech, another conversation even—one which answered indirectly, tangentially, to the music I had heard all my life. The lateness of that change seems embarrassing to me now, until I remember that it grew out of something I could not have wished earlier: a death, and thus an absence, which left me to make new arrangements.

The curious verbal form that is called poetry, however disposed on the page, is perhaps, at some level, always a re-arrangement of the silence left by the past—by the dead we know, and those we don't. One of my own early poems, written soon after that Christmas and published years later in my first, tentative volume, tries to catch, in small scale, the compass of that quiet, as well as the exchange it invited. As things turned out, it too would not be a last word.

Spills

These splinty yellows, greens—short straws
stooked in a clear glass—suddenly stop me
    dead, remembering:

fire, the catch of it live—the whet
and lick fetched to your pipe and embering
    breath rings.

A whipcrack, flick, and the sparks winked
starry-eyed just for a split-second, tacked
    on the coal-black.

Spills made spells. We never guessed
their wish and flash might also slow-fuse
    quick to death.

A lump in my throat, seeing them there.
Spillikins, child's play. Yours, the pipe-dreams.
    Mine, cold spells.

Life from Sixteen Angles

Poems

A Stay

I've laid a cradle of sticks. Too late. But stay.
A spider picks the heartstrings of its web.
Why this should even matter's hard to say,

or why ash wood's for lighting late in the day.
Across the face of things an intricate rib
of twist extends. What makes it stick and stay?

My spills lie crosswise, haywire, like a game you'd play.
A spider plucks dream-notes and spreads its hub.
Why this should even matter's hard to say.

It's lightfoot, lighter than news and worlds away
as if your ear might register, ad lib,
its texting step, tremolo, its spidery stay.

So catch it. What? Like sound from the thread's piqué,
cradled deep in the network's growing nub,
a thought too far to reach, too hard to say.

Then ash to ashes—a match will light the way.
That spider tweaks the fibres of its web.
Pausing, I think: build patterns, make a stay.
Why should this even matter? Hard to say.

Pen Nibs: In Memoriam

'because a thought itself possesses a water pattern.'
– Joseph Brodsky

Scritch, scritch—busy rats in the sewers,
their script, rough scratchings,

and I, at the old shop long boarded up
where once I bought

job-lots of discontinued pen nibs,
their metal pinches,

inking prongs, rusting in heaps
where nightly the high tide

needled the brickwork, nibbling ashore
in a practised catastrophe,

and all the drowning finery of our lives
went dreaming under

aqua alta in the night of the past,
leaving a green

(cyane, verdigris) watermark of weed,
like something you'd read

of events long ago or of no great moment,
decipherable hints

of lives now finished, works unachieved,
while a rat in the sewer

goes scritch, scritch—and a litmus of light
shines where I

no longer acquire tray-loads of pen nibs,
but listen for you

where a weedy tide-line left by the sea's
seasonal notation

shapes feather nibs on cipollino water,
like pen to paper.

Deerpark

Unhunted now, these lightweight rangers trip
  so winning, fleet
in the cool of the evening, quick and uppity, feet

like rainfall's downfall, hooves that shape and pitch
  ellipses on grass . . .
grace notes over gravity's ground bass.

Footing

for Subha

Poor worn beasts—*feet*—are they mine? Queer things,
bearing an uprightness on calibrated bones,
footworn in footwear, cooped all winter through,
poor brutes, their palmy feelers shuttered in dark shoes—
now freed and mushroom-pale, eerie as moons.

Do toes—ten stunted fingers—miss their hold?
their dreamed, prehensile lives among the trees,
their adept grip aboveground, branching clear
as if to handle heights, easy as air?
Now their skills are all for staying below.

So far from me they seem, bare flaps, shy tramps,
small scales to take my weight and forwardness
(from footling breach to feet-first through the door).
Their measure's just a step. *Steady on!* I say.
They'll keep me earthed, these groundlings, on the way.

A Limestone Pavement

Tarn—perhaps Old Norse for *tear.*
It overflows, goes under quick
at Water Sinks, filtering its flow—
who knows how deep? So earth might sieve
the stream of sorrow under our feet
and limestone turn an eye as cold
as this cold comfort: losing our hold

over quirky fissures, clints and grykes
where hart's tongue fern, dog mercury
tease a life from obscure vents—
who knows how deep? (*Lacrimae rerum.*)
Up here, bone-white, this calcified lace
is child's hopscotch over the abyss,
dance-steps chiselled over what we miss.

Docklands

Those steely skeletons crowd, locked to the sky,
or stoop, heartless, to a foreign border.
       Water's a relief.

We step off-shore, on board, and quickly feel
the sough and thump of waves, a dance floor
       under our feet,

while gantries, derricks, cranes recede in the mist,
container trucks and trains, grain-chutes
       of chaff and meal,

and here and there, anywhere on the rough dockside,
an abandoned warehouse ghosts its rooms—
       nothing to contain.

From Naples, Leith, Hull—now Gdansk (Westerplatte)—
this pulling away in the driving rain
       opens a gap

where the grey wash swivels and drains, rounding fast
in waste, derivative pools. What sinks
       in that sluice or wake?

Our feet touch shiplap boards, a hugger-mugger beat,
feel wave-shifts counter, lurch and strain,
       upsetting the rule

as a 'drunken sailor' tune rollicks in Polish,
and the whole sturdy dock-side slides
       wide from where—

we're out, clear, in the talking wind and sea,
leaving that gear, those giant pins'
    filigree mechanism

faded to rain's writing in the long back view.
Day's dusk begins. We're headed far out,
    where sea closes in.

Sea Ears

Painter, sister, what is it you perceive?—
the sea's refractive index, blue to green,

shot stuff, *sfumato* tints, solutions of colour—
those twisted undercurrents, travelling weather?

It hems a shifting selvage, scallops an edge,
scatters its fancywork for easy pickings:

slipper limpet, tellin, spindle shell,
common winkle, whelk or wendletrap,

Mr Whippy shapes, the beach's freebies
ruched and whorled like frosted goffering—

each ambulacrum, emptied to a hum
some tiny muscle tongued when it was in,

each cavity, a hall that trumpets sea
till sea returns to fetch its tendered debris.

The Anatomy Lecture, by Rembrandt

'a cool scientist, almost an algebraist, in the service of a subtle dreamer'
– Paul Valéry

The painter sits full square, unsparing,
sizing up the slump of the thing,
its weight of muscle, pigmentation of skin,
its cold set, and naked pity.

Someone has trowelled as far as the heart,
eviscerating the movable parts.
That brutal cavity draws you in
to darkness, arched as a butcher's carcass.

The feet seem live still, ticklish, touching,
hands too big, fallen slack by the way.
A man with a bowl to catch sudden spills
ponders, inwardly, this gutted pietà.

Closed eyes, dropped chin, a shifted hairline—
he might be sleeping, lost to the world.
The unhurt face looks meditative,
relaxed even, till you search above

where someone has prised the lock of the skull.
Did he crack it? taking hammer and chisel
to the fontanelles, forcing their dovetails,
lifting their cover to discover what's within?

Consider. Don't wince. With fork or scalpel
he picks over the matter in hand,
extrudes a thread of subtle feeling,
plucks a bare nerve, twines a dream-strand

to draw the secret of that infinite coil
from frontal lobe or cerebral cortex—
the lost soul of an intricate housing,
slippy, covert, on a hiding to nowhere,

or nowhere you'd know. The anatomist still
plies the thick of matter for the thought
of thought's own workings—wish or trigger,
twist or chip that fired the brainwave.

But the painter catches something flown
from the skull's packed nest, its ransacked privacy:
a dream of thinking, fancy's flight,
and touches, brushing it half to life,

as if to say: look close at this stuff,
the miracle of its solving mechanism.
I give you, transacted, exactly its measure:
dream and engine, once fleshed together.

Below-Stairs

Houseroom for things you forget or try to imagine:
a saw, two planks of plywood, jam jar of nails,
the shredded fibres of a doormat returning to hair,
coal scuttle, pair of breathless bellows—
implements in their places—for love, for sorrow,
and something immeasurably near, nudging the hardware.

It's where you put things, see? Out of sight, on hold.
They wait, unredeemed, unclaimed for decades or more
where a windless chronic air lags and corrodes.
Is it in there, still? that ancient, reflex scare?
a dream of hiding, trapped under infinite stairs,
bolthole for never quite knowing no-one's there

except oneself, fooled in childhood fears?—
unless, even so (yird-hunger rooting for the cold
where last we found them, stored among signs and wonders,
holed among rusty tools, wincy spiders . . .)
somehow we'd know, in that indoor earthy closeness,
a sudden glory: their answering, lonely faces.

Childhood's pit of dares, daredevil's den,
cache of keeps and losses, teases, thrills—
a creep of outdoor damp in the flaking walls,
a broken concrete floor caking to soil.
Open the door a crack and you smell it still,
below-stairs air, too near, too close to home.

Lullaby

It seemed a croon or charm: *night night, sleep tight.*
Her wide eyes fought to keep the darkness out.
Yet something far and wide came in by right,
creeping, as if she knew it all the while

behind the easy tune of adult lies.
It doubled, echoing; it told in time,
until the bluff of darkness on her eyes
disclosed how close, how endless, that *night night.*

Blown Bubble, in Variable Time

Slower than you'd think—
(blown . . . here)—a thin, circumstantial O,
a globe adrift with earth tones,
      hedge and road
mirrored, if you look, shivered in a caul
of water colour, weightless, marbly floater—
      like a thought come by.

Lighter than you'd know—
(blown . . . where?)—a clear, aspirant O,
omega, turned and flown,
      riding the thermals,
showing, if you look, in its compound eye
a planet's passing colours, passing sky—
      like grieving, why?

Quicker than you'd wish—
(blown . . . far)—a shy, diaphanous O,
shine in the day's dullness,
      light-bowled rainbow
lasting, if you look, no longer than this:
its copious, quivering world shot to the finish—
      like wishing, to cry.

Composition: To a Wine-Glass of Water
for John

Steady, hard by the window, you might see through it,
this glass of air and water, lighter than colour.
Its thin stem blooms a nearly invisible flower.

Observe how light abstracts in the compass of its vent
where a pencil-line circles an inner circle.
A lucid solution settles its clear content.

Yet a cup of nearly nothing is ear's work too:
pavilion of rings, *glissando* at the touch of skin,
a hum chambered in a fine curve, drawn from its hiding.

So slide a finger across its all-clear, riffle
the rim—it turns harmonic. Stroke that high note
till the pitch, unlocked from its crystal, *says* something.

But knocked, no longer in the grip of form, it spills,
dashed to splinters, puddles, chips of the middle-
distance, broken bits. That fall, a soundprint,

puzzles the floor. Nothing you'd find to salvage—
unless, look again: the shattered physic of a bell,
a call recalled in passing, funny aquarelle.

November Song

Spelling it out on the phone I pause, and say:
    N for November.
An apt address, I think, open to all:
All Saints, All Souls—my postcode's posthumous.
Out there in seasonless space they hold their peace.
Our planetary weather's far beyond their reach.

Then why, writing, did I touch a stranger place?
    (*profundo lacu.*)
My slippy pen, mis-spelling, made the change:
not *Sharon*, from sun and soil, but *Charon fruit*—
the old rower of souls bringing golden globes,
lights from the unlit straits, dim proofs or probes—

November's fruits returned by the ferry load,
    late sweets, lost code.
The season's closing dark attracts such gold—
long luminous recalls from foreign fields.
Now all my crowded gathering dead come in,
hard on the head of a name, a slip of the pen.

Sluice

It's pitch and sudden in a brick siding.
Toadflax and stonecrop shiver in a draught—
precarious frills whiskering the brickwork,
tickling a shaft that dives to the dark

where an old cellar-smell wells up from a drain,
where walls contain the whisk and tarry
of blacker water, and a gate regulates
its Stygian takings, drop by drop.

We stop to watch a swallow draw
wish-lists of hills on the fossed flats,
where stacked mops of reed-mace make
populous outcrops, heads above us.

Below, a sluice-grid monitors the flow.
Water queues in straight dug channels,
where all its leafy detritus scums
in unmoved pools, in pausing stills—

till quick and under, a black coil of wet
sucks through the fipple of a blade.
We watch the runaway water swell
in undercurrents to the shining levels.

Crocus

i.m. Anne Barton, Trinity College

'l'animo nostro informe . . . come un croco'
[our formless spirit . . . like a crocus]
– Montale

From Hebrew, *Karkom*, Arabic, *Kurkum*—
once, she asked me: are the crocuses out?
Come spring, who'll walk that terrestrial ground?

Night after night her high lit windows
signed the passing weather of the sky.
Now they're dark, heights clarify.

The scholar's gain and loss contend
beyond the Court's palaestra of lawn,
through windy arches where the river bends.

Christopher Wren or Christopher Robin—
will some bird carry us over the Cam
to the crocus fields, to see them again?

It's late. I plant six bulbs in a ring.
My soil's small-holding holds them in
and makes a handsel, though it weighs deadweights.

Lines at Break of Day

Remembering Isaac Rosenberg

So quiet, now, in early slanting sun,
the day so young we might not have happened yet,
the garden clear of us, history unbegun.

We might be conceived afresh, new-chanced for life,
not guilty, used—in hindsight none the wiser,
in foresight only blinder for all our news.

Turning, I catch a gleam, the lightest thread
thrown to the winds, slack yet holding fast,
a shine-conductor wiring a poppy to a post.

Then everywhere, that spidery filigree rigging,
so many ligaments of hair, hair's-breadth, short lengths
to take the open measure of what's not there.

From flower to fence, from walnut tree to wall
these web filaments uphold a world in fall,
erect a scaffolding in autumn air.

Just a trick of the eye perhaps, a shot of magic—
but look, and you track a fibre-optic line
of light, sideways, to catch the sun in passing;

then nothing, or something again, a fluke travelling
even as you turn, till lost to view—a sensor
sensing your presence, a lightly glancing answer.

Lines, like others, so fragile, bound, once learned
by the book, by ear, fibres of a remembered sound—
lines, like tiny consistencies crossing the gap

between this and that—lines that carry, connect
and seem like nothing, a wish perhaps, and yet
a tether, a hold on things, a kind of sense.

They cannot stay a poppy or staunch a hurt,
parry a gunshot, stop a threat or tank—
or cure, or expiate. They only hang

like strung telegraphs of light, slides of shimmer—
reminders of life again at break of day:
new chance, a start—given, fragile, and unmeant.

Roundel for the Children

A toytown compound
(here we go round, here we go round),
for a time safe on the inside, primed
to practise falling down the long slide
    into a sandpit,
or gallop, pillion, on a bucking legless horse,
seats like raised hackles (listen,
    Kinderszenen into *Kyrie*),
or spin faster than pushed, and fling
clean out of orbit—then back to beginning.

We'll cover old ground
(here we go round, here we go round)
for a time safe on the outside, set-aside,
watching them play, a dare for a ride
    into the future.
For others, elsewhere, a lasting skirl or keen,
our Childermas wailing in the wings
    (*eleison eleison*).
Those go airborne beyond us and swing
into their big skies—then back to beginning.

Capriform

No kidding!
    Goat with its old coat on—
stinky renegade in rags and tatters—
      you'd think
the devil of a thing in beggar's wear

        or

      footsure loafer, stone-sifter,
savvy rogue—
        for pity's sake
maybe the desert landscape's scapegoat
    wearing our hate.

69388

'I played Schumann's *Träumerei* for Dr Mengele.'
  – Anita Lasker-Wallfisch

Gut-sick   I stroke   exact
        peg-stretched   catgut
cattle-stamped   I stop   double-stop
        legered   notes
report   into air where   ash smoke
        disports   those blown
spacey   skymen   rising
        stoked   in a plume.

Dreamed   by line   by sheer
        number   totting
up stop   I think   double-stopping
        strings   in his hear-
ing stop   heart-stop-   ping
        listen   you could drop
dead   living   numbered
        I play   to the ending

Poems

Rosin

This lucent gum's
brittle nub
bleb of amber
vegetable blood

nugget of gold
warm palm-crosser
stroked by a bow
drawn to an ear

honed and grainy
combed by horsehair
as if I stroked
frankincense or myrrh

and found in the snicked
trunk of a slash pine
colophony
or a strange girl's name.

This brush with matter
a live tree wept
touching stuff
like honey wood-let

lends a curious
crystal tear
for the reach of a sound
that will melt on air

and calls across
centuries of waste
mortling dumps
mass-graves dead-meat

till one hurt tree
speaks to the hurt
and a bone music
bites in each note.

Crystal

He'll cut a cylinder piece, mould a parison.
Sand and limestone heat at 1000 degrees.
Liquefactions deflect
in a red-hot furnace—genesis, birthing sacs—

then stack together on the dead-plate, set and cool,
tested for checks or stones, blisters or tears,
flaws in the ware.
Who knows how many, failed, have been lost or crushed?

I lift this glass to the light. It scoops a sky.
The glaze is clear and glancing (apocryphal stuff),
as if a dancer
shaped in reverse the air that frames her there.

Cup for a cup-bearer, chalice for water—
this phial's ambient curve, its spirit level
tipped by gravity,
is fragile. Handle with care. I raise it higher

to catch in the light of nothing, something here.
Life's crystal holds, skin-deep, and cups its chance.
Elsewhere, *listen hard*,
the shot, bomb-blitz, the fission—shattered glass.

Dump

'Somewhere they must have gone . . .'
– Isaac Rosenberg

An extramural spot walled in by wires—
    so why,
criss-crossed, cross-checked, might a gusty no-man's wind
blow liberally across that line? We're in.
    Outside,
the planed and level lands are nowhere far.
The headroom's trimmed with stripes and spiked with barbs.

Some things end here, quilted, sorted together—
    a clown's
scrapheap, collectibles fallen in lots:
white goods, wood fittings, paper, chemicals, electrics,
    set-asides
set in sidings, our saved and graded waste.
So much is ours, now full of absentness.

A trench of motley shows its patchwork of lives—
    mixed piles
of clothes, *soul-sacks*, discarded intimacies
gutted and heaped like guys, poor absentees,
    like signs
of what's not here to haunt our eyes.
Which clown's assorted losses must we stand by?

Dump—a place to guard, a word ... *Who hurled*
    them out?—
their one-time ripeness massing in a grave of scraps.
This camp of parts—where a stranger's dress, wind-lashed,
    is trapped
akimbo on the wires—exacts an epitaph:
for pity, pity, unearthing war's deep pits.

Poems

'Aftermath: Parasite'

for Maggi Hambling

What's this? War work? So call it 'Aftermath'.
All flesh is grass. The second mowing's art.

A broken torso strung to its carrying cross,
wood-nymph or totem, curious nubby boss,

stickler, unsightly gobbet, raw impress,
a newborn fledgling set to fly the nest,

a touching kiss in two-step, *pas de deux*,
meat-hook or metastasis, *faute de mieux*,

the stuff of life, parasite or specimen case,
the heart itself coupled to heights and base,

an instrument fine-strung from root-stock wood,
accord and touch, a sound not understood:

this human foreign body flush on its log,
a stranger metaphored, the finger of God.

Epistolary

I've written all my life along narrow lines,
rules that show the way from this to that.

I've touched the lips of letters, sent a kiss
winging in time across immeasurable miles.

@talktalk.net no distance nets them now.
My *send* receives *mail error* in reply.

Then one by one, each year, my dead addressees,
deleted, leave no record, return no sign.

Santa, the child once begged, by letter, by fire.
Dear Christ, I curse, on the quick updraught of a prayer.

On the Fridge Magnets

No help! unless, buttoning a blank,
badging the sheer white falls of it,
these gubbins, woubits, whigmaleeries—
clamped to the iron draw of its north,
pressed to the cold collateral flat—
might pose a prayer, entreat for relief,
each magnet's pin-up a *magnificat*.

What's to do? These bright bought things,
tagged truisms, riffs or rhymes
baffle the lonely whites of its sides,
hang small hopes like trophies won.
(Imagine the hum that beats in humdrum,
the calling wolf that sings in a cantaloup,
rain's calligraphy, a calligram.)

Unless those heartening phrases cry
(the unmoved fridge-god keeping his cool)
just for this: for the crying-out-loud's sake,
think them cheap-jack hustlers in a space,
attention-mongers cadging for more,
and all their addresses, like prisoners' knocks,
a tacky *vox clamantis* on the door.

Nativity

Between this and that, an ox and an ass,
chanced at twilight in the solstice cold,
static, between-times, a star comes out—
star-fooled I pause, *entre chien et loup.*

And pick my way, now dark underfoot,
half-lost, half-home, in the world's old fall.
An owl brushes my blindness by.
Nights are the clearest sights of all.

The glamour of it, new snow, sub-zero,
dazzling rebuff, a baffle on the land—
éclaircissements, neiges d'antan—
my long memory minds, and minds:

how once all feather-stitched with ice
a window lanced its look of sky,
and useful water petrified—
between this and that, a time to die.

Easterly

At the ninth hour. Jesus, the cold!
And a small dashed clown, off-course, exhausted—
splaycd orange feet and a short wing-span,
flung by weather too strong for weathering—
    badges the cliff-top.
Was it too much for him, driven in a cross-wind, storm-tossed?

At the ninth hour. So the story goes.
And nothing to ease the old wound of cold
but this bright jester on a rocky landing—
his white eye-shadow camp and curious,
    tweaked for laughter,
and the beak's painted rainbow blazing after.

    Old pal, sweet puffin!
are you dead for nothing at the edge of the world?
flowered on the grass where no flowers grow?
Good Friday's cold seems colder for
    these colours spilled—
and the wind, icy for March, still easterly, kills.

Canticles for a Passion

THE GARDEN

What was it, then, that thing
    under the skin?
splinter or spell? wood-chip?
    I might nit-pick
but it's in, niggling, and will take
    slow drawing—

the wood's intimate invasion,
    landing quick
in my finger, prick in the flesh,
    nip in the skin-tight
rigging of my hand, gardening,
    digging in.

A clutch of twigs, the cradled fall-out from a gust of wind,
rough splints, spindles or withies, pencils or spills—

whatever they are, just a cross-hatched arrangement of space and air,
an architecture of accidentals, an absence addressed—

like a rook's nest, rock-a-bye high in a lacework of trees,
or a child's scribble, erasing the face that was smiling beneath—

as if you discerned the spirit caught in a crucifixion of sticks,
or else the soul, blown like smoke from its bone kindling.

Poems: Canticles for a Passion

And he came out, and went, as he was wont, to the
Mount of Olives . . . (LUKE 22:39)

Somewhere among the trees I'll find you.

Their wooden company
                yours for the asking—
rough but live
                rooted but branching
their oil a balm
                their trunks a stay
in the night watches
                with only the breathing
sleepers by
                and the moon's large coin
shifting away.

You is a name I'm searching for.

The olive trees are yours.

✳

He went forth with his disciples over the brook Cedron,
where was a garden . . . (JOHN 18:1)

Trees in the garden stand like guards,
fanciful totems
of an agony unwound—
olives dwarfed by centuries of drought,
their twisted hardwood
thickened from growth rings, boled and gnarled,
bowed down in gravity's tether
yet bearing loads
of sky and weather.

Trees might listen, rooted and still,

players too in the winds that come,
their gaping hollows
cracked and split, knotted and slant,
as if a sprite
might just step out
(wood-wose, wood-nymph),
and leave in the curve of each wood-cut
a shape that's human.

＊

*And he cast down the pieces of silver in the temple, and
departed, and went and hanged himself. [...] And they took
counsel, and bought with them the potter's field, to bury
strangers in.* (MATT. 27: 5, 7)

Who goes there? Who knows? Not yet the crowd,
the rabble, rough types, firebrands, and that
Iscariot, the odd one, the unconvinced—
bad egg, or victim of a universal plan.

Not yet the waking, the lights, the arrest,
lifted sword or proffered kiss—
the way a story had to go, like this,
leaving its print in the words we know.

Not yet his money bags flung on the floor,
the tainted sum, the change of heart,
regret, shame, a tree and a rope—
not yet the strangers in the potter's field

buried in stone, rubble and brick,
throwaway stuff, discarded crocks,
and all the despairing who could not bear
the shame they carried, the grief they lived.

✄

You is a presence wide spaces shape—
like stepping out in a spangle of starlight,
profligate, yet shedding no light
on this garden of shadows, valley of night,

where an owl witters, forgetting its long lines,
and moonshine polishes a polythene sack
of rotting silage, catching its gleam
like cat's-eyes in headlights, a shiny wetlook.

A silver piece, a song of sixpence,
that lunar disc in a field of sparks.
The dark's obtuse and palpable
from owls' time till the rising of larks.

The night is friendless, the sleepers clapped out.
Quiet creates a shadow-play of trees.
Wood-notes repeat a story long known.
You is a presence my hearing sees.

✄

*Did I not see thee in the garden with him? Peter then denied
again: and immediately the cock crew.* (JOHN 18: 26-27)

The garden is still. The hour not yet
when a maid will draw water, the workers withdraw,
and a man walk away, blinded by tears

for a dream disproved, a world betrayed,
himself, untrue—and the cockerel's mock-
repartee forever now crowing in his ears.

✄

Rooster, coxcomb, strut your stuff,
quick-march, finicky, across the yard,
cocky fellow, waking cantor,
waiting your moment, keeping faith
with light's first light, day's new day.

Hey you! beautiful, simple and unsaved,
small king of this world, this patch of ground
scratched for a living with fingery claws.
You'll feed, crap, mate, sleep,
fight for your own life, no questions asked.

Lord of the morning, king of the sun—
arouser, dream-dispeller, small clock,
reality-check when the night's a terror,
heart-stopper, too, if we stop to look.
Peter, through tears, heard: *I know not, I know not.*

Foolish man; the maid shrugged him off.
The workers edged away from the fire—
another trial, another long day.
The cat pounced, and missed altogether.
That cock shuffled an iridescence of feathers.

✗

It's quiet in the garden. *Shh!* not a sound . . . or is it a twig
fallen to the ground, a rat scuffling, dog barking,
perhaps a sparrow fidgeting for nits? or the sap of a tree

rising, rising, the planet adjusting its turn in space,
its light brush against a star-struck vacuum?—or else, perhaps,
a sleeper catching his breath in a dream—an angel, landing?

Poems: Canticles for a Passion

And there followed him a great company of people, and of women,
which also bewailed and lamented him. (LUKE 23:27)

The usual crowd:
soldiers, loafers, street vendors,
mourners, preachers, a riff-raff
of idlers, gawpers, foreigners

caught in the flow,
drawn to the thing on the road
out of town, out beyond the walls
with the dust, the dogs, the outlawed.

It's always the same:
roughing it under the sun,
foot-slogging, looking for something:
a thrill, a sorrow, a calling,

following anyway
to see each criminal done in
the Roman way, upped and staked
akimbo, human-shaped.

—⋆—

The long road out's the one you have to take.
It's always unsafe.
A shanty, a siding, some straggling suburb's industrial estate,
past the gasworks,
the brickworks, a littered wasteland, polluted sump,
out along
a disused railway, landfill site,
by a travellers' camp,
migrants' caravans, on out past
the last signpost, the end of signposts:
by an avenue of tombs, a garden wall—
it's the way you must come.

＞＜

And he bearing his cross went forth into a place called the place
of a skull . . . (JOHN 19:17)

No way, you'd think? Not for you, that route?
Those dream-struck fellows scarpered, too.
Where were they at the end?
Peter weeping, Judas hanged.
The rest in hiding from the law, themselves—
confederates of a common criminal,
friends of the condemned.

Then there was only John, the lover,
and the women, the mother . . .
Forget it. Go home. This is no way to come.

＞＜

they laid hold upon one Simon, a Cyrenian, coming out of
the country . . . (LUKE 23:26)

Bad luck, old chap. You've drawn the short one.
Heave to. Help out. You've got strong shoulders.
We don't want this wretch to die on the road.
Hitch up and take the tail end, come!
We need to move on, stop this log-jam.

＞＜

Simon of Cyrene, crossed by chance,
in the wrong place at the wrong time.
Simon the listener, the Libyan, the stranger,
picked on, hauled out, just passing that way:
I do not know, I do not know the man.
(The other Simon's nowhere to be found.)

＞＜

Poems: Canticles for a Passion

For if they do these things in a green tree, what shall be done in the dry? (LUKE 23:31)

It's a weight of wood fit to take a man,
high as the topmast that will sail new seas,
strong as the crossbeam that will steady a house,
straight as the pole that telegraphs a fear.

But Simon, for you it's an ache, a bruise,
a chip on the shoulder, stigma driven in,
a splinter lodged deep under the skin.
You'll draw it later. Life goes on.

So which is the way? *Quo vadis,* stranger?
What's your business? Where do you live?
Have you a visa, papers, proof?
Jew or gentile? Your age, your race?

Simon of Cyrene, father of two sons,
arrived from a journey—the rest, unknown.
Bystander, caught up, touched, untouched,
part of a story. Nothing to do with him.

The way's an interval between this and that, a space for
an outing, a ramble, a rout, perhaps a pilgrimage, more
like a picnic—the crowd mixing its assortment of lives,
jostling, joking, policed and curbed—but no children
here, not yet for them, the rough ending, those grisly
scarecrows hung on their sticks—and stray dogs snarl-
ing, their eyes on a titbit, a bag, a wrapper, snapping
when they're kicked—and the women, different, out of
their element, jeered and catcalled, elbowed and shoved,
struggling to carry water, towels, struggling to keep up—
and the dusty road going on and on, stony, potholed,
faint in a heat-haze, too far to contemplate, too near to
think, the whole thing dragging inch by inch, with a load
of wood, a weight of pain, the way you must come . . .

＊

Now there stood by the cross of Jesus his mother, and his mother's
sister, Mary the wife of Cleophas, and Mary Magdalene.
(JOHN 19:25)

The mother stands
beside a son

for those who hold
dead children in their arms

those who nightly
plead and mourn

whose work of birth
is terribly wasted

making and breaking
birthing and earthing.

The mother stands
beside a tree

its wood a gallows
its strength a rack

centuries-old
centuries-long

how long to wait?
her grief a stand

her life a question:
no answer to it.

What was it, then, that thing?
        saddled with dirt,
riddling my trowel's sharp blade?
    I dig down and find
that it's loose, puzzling, and will take
        slow polishing.

Treasure buried in earth
        amid bulbs and roots,
chips and scraps and potsherds,
        detritus and decay:
the moon's dropped sixpence
        for what it's worth.

*Now in the place where he was crucified there was a garden; and
in the garden a new sepulchre . . .* (JOHN 19:41)

So quiet, so dark, you must see with your ears.
Was it the same road out, or another?
So early—*ssst!*—not even a bird
shifts in its sleep, not even a leaf,

only a scuffed stone under your feet
cracks as you pass, flips like the first
heartbeat in the universe—or is it the last?
Flowers at your feet, passion or pasque.

Now upon the first day of the week, very early in the morning,
they came unto the sepulchre, bringing the spices which they
had prepared . . . (LUKE 24:1)

In the cool of the morning, at first light of day—
it's the last chance (two days gone by),
and it's women's work, cradle to grave,

to bring unguents, oils, sweet spices, myrrh,
to touch and wash, anoint, caress,
to hold and know the perished stuff

stopped in the earth, soiled and shut,
to go where you'd rather not, to cross
over—into that hell again.

⋇

Feel this earth
under your feet,
its mould, clay,
grit, peat,
tilth that turns
to plough or spade,
deep as darkness,
heavy as grief.

Touch this base
of earth, under-earth,
roots and tubers,
seeds and spores,
the soil that feeds
life in the upper air,
then receives
each to its underworld.

Poems: Canticles for a Passion

✳

And the napkin, that was about his head, not lying with
the linen clothes, but wrapped together in a place by
itself. (JOHN 20:7)

And then that joke, that detail—funny thing!
the place empty, the stone rolled off—
was it an error or a dazzling theft?—
and the women, bereft.

Had they come the wrong way, to the wrong garden,
mistaken the grave?
Whose trick was this, whose master-stroke?
grave-robbers, body-snatchers,
a political ruse?

And then that joke, the folded linen,
first the headpiece, then the rest—

was it a clue or else a decoy?
who had stopped to tidy the stuff?—

as if someone rose
from a bed of terrors,

removed his night-clothes
one by one,

shedding those habits,
unwinding those bands,

taking the time
to pause, and fold

his laundry, neatly,
like a guest who'll be gone . . .

or was it a whim
of the teller's tale

to imagine how long
he might have lingered—

unwilling, undressing,
watching, savouring,

making a stay—
then dead or away?

✳

She, supposing him to be the gardener. . . (JOHN 20:15)

The gardener stands very still. He listens, waits.
    He might be a shadow, might be a tree.
Mistaking's easy in the dim beginning of the morning—
first light, barely even light, and an early bird
    trying its notes, tuning.

The gardener stands very still. He waits, listens.
    Birds of the air, flowers of the field
are known to him. The time's not yet. Later he will
dig over, plant out, stake in, pot on, pinch out.
    He handles living, and dead things.

The gardener belongs in the garden. He figures there.
    He'll turn loose clods, scatter new seed.
He senses rain, attends the law of the sun.
The planter, cutter, mower, old harrower of subsoil,
    this man goes under, and above.

✳

Poems: Canticles for a Passion

Half-light half-dark
                    a world in doubt
no trusting your eyes
                    no knowing the way
between dog and wolf
                    dead or alive

till shades realise
                    their bulk and shape
at the brink and turn
                    of planet to sun
at the pause before
                    the birds return

and branches hold
                    the sky of a new day
like wiry giants
                    caryatids
carrying the dawn
                    on outstretched limbs.

✁

Then arose Peter, and ran unto the sepulchre; and stooping down,
he beheld the linen clothes laid by themselves, and departed,
wondering . . . (LUKE 24:12)

Here in the garden of supposition,
in the furtive light of a dawning calm
found after toil and long attrition,

a small surmise, hunger or wish,
perhaps like nothing but deepened wonder
at a tale reheard: at the listening hush

of that working figure, mysterious gardener—
that slip, mistaking, the story's surprise.
Someone waits, between truth and error.

✳

And while they yet believed not for joy, and wondered . . .
(LUKE 24:41)

It's quiet in the garden, so quiet you'd hear
    the trees growing:
sap in the trunk, creak in the woodwork,
push of a root foraging beneath,
aspiration of an unopened shoot,

or sigh of a dryad stirring in heartwood—
    the string stretched
between bridge and peg, screw and rack,
sound-post set between belly and back,
this body of the thing—the music it makes.

The Slipper Chapel

Soon you'll shed the pacing rhythm of the way,
unshackle ties you had no choice to make.
Was it this road, or another you meant to take?
No matter. Here ends death march or pilgrimage.

You might have needed simples as you went:
self-heal, heart's-ease, speedwell, forget-me-not.
They helped for a time, but could not cure foot-rot,
heart-ache, gut-retch, the lingering fester of despair.

It was always lonely, though millions passed on the road.
Most of the time you missed the world you crossed
on by-ways, sidetracks, turnabouts—born for lost.
You start from who you are, and walk and walk.

Now pause. Ease off those boots. Unsock sore feet.
Slip out of time that beat to help you find
the road ahead, already left behind.
You're done. No prize for this. Life slips out of mind.

Diversion

Just when we thought we were almost there, home and
dry, that yellow signpost sent us sharp off, down a steep
hill to a narrow lane, ash and elder on either side, no
blackthorn in flower or early daffodils, just the bony
winter undress of those trees, and the ground strewn
with windblown twigs that crunched under the wheels,
till soon we were no longer diverted at all, but making
wrong choices at every unmarked turn and junction
where, lost for signs, fooled, bewildered, we drove hope-
lessly on and on, and emerged at last among open fields,
clods of shine turned mutely to the sky, the earthy marl
sleek and blank, harrowed deeply, and saw, looking up:

　that thing propped in the middle of a field, stick-manikin
in a flap of rags, that dressed affliction, a shilpit sick bogle
or golem, rigged up, stuffed with windlestraw, stretched
and tortured with espaliered arms;

　unless what it was—lost on a road we'd long given up on,
lost to ourselves, destination missed and map discarded—
was not some grisly, lop-headed mock, some daft puck or
crutched, splint-crossed, staked mommet with a shock of
limbs,

　but the whole point and joke of it finally, the last straw,
our roundabout homing nowhere on earth, but fallen
out among twigs and withies, clods and harrows, till face
to face with that thing, that clown, our own silly laugh-
ing look-alike, erect and bare: the resurrection's scare.

By the Fire

Shh! Funny thing. Sometimes it sings.
Rose-bloom turns dust-grey as it dies.
Flames trash their gold of lives
while the soul, finessed to a wavering fumarole,
soars, out of breath . . . A kind of wit,
to leave and climb—sky's the limit.

Too light, volatile. What's left behind
is clink and hush, witter and sigh,
ash to ashes where the flames subside
and soot scintillates in constellations.
Conceive the soul: puff and exit,
wish, residue,—*et resurrexit.*

Even-Song

'that roar which lies on the other side of silence.'
– George Eliot

Something wants in.
Who'll mourn by halves
the vacuum quiet
of a slew of stars
and the moon's thin
shifting anchor
crux and mover
fascinator.

Out in the woods
is owlscope's scare
(you don't look there).
How would stars sound
if you could hear?
From old provençale
(call it a prayer)
le gai saber.

We belong in the calends
of accountable days.
Our currency's air.
Its obstacle carries
breakthrough soundwaves.
(My love in the desert
of a fatal regret
turns blind and deaf.)

Yet something wants in.
A moth, is it?
flutter-tonguing the pane
the dead still beckoning.
We're bound to this
perpetual audition
this second-hearing
of a silent thing.

Now mourn by halves.
A slow coronach
through darkened glass
sings the after-
silence that must start.
Like roaring starlight
(unimaginable din) . . .
something wants in.

Playing for Chopin

So many dry stone walls might halt a landfall,
cadenzas of weather in winter, alluvial rains

that wreck the terracing, leach the reclaimed levels
of olives, oranges, vines—their livings' ledgers.

Cold. I remember the cold, and clouds come down
too quick, muting the sheep-bells when flocks move on—

transhumant wanderers calling from worlds away.
The valley's deep auditorium carries the sound.

Here the museum's too quiet, enclosing its own.
What touching compulsion draws me back to that room,

back to his piano, *Pleyel* (to play the fool),
while air, an audience, clairaudient, almost an ear,

bends close—cat's-whisker to the silent notes?
Someone's left a red rose flecking the keyboard.

There are photos, portraits, letters, manuscript papers,
voices of children elsewhere, in empty cloisters

where the monks' old pharmacy displays its simples, arts;
outside, a log-pile stacks and honeycombs the dark.

I'm thinking: Opus 28. These ivory keys
are touchy as fingers, easy as opening doors,

a palmistry for feeling how a memorised wish
might still transmit, hand-to-hand, his time to this.

But the sound's long gone. Rattled, the slack strings cough.
A shocked resonance trails tunelessly off.

Outside, first raindrops; a thick mist hushes the air.
Far off, otherworldly, those sheep-bells call and answer.

A Little Poem for a Space

Anywhichway it goes, friend,
poetry happens and makes it so,
in the taste of a sound that's said, in the time
it takes, just whiling itself away—

as stopped, any day, on the hiatus of a bridge
(willows' branch-lines trailing on water,
precision nibs tracking on paper,
phrases crossed from another conversation)—

till a leaping fish (bright curve, queered light,
articulate locksmith braced in its scales)
cuts like Persephone's bracelet, imparts
abstraction of argent, ringed from the dark.

Pomegranate

'he said that she might return to earth if she had not taken
any food in the infernal regions.'
 – Lemprière, *Classical Dictionary*

First, the scent of fennel in the air,
inflammable stalks of a dried-out summer,
Etna's spills, god's gift of fire,
and the cicadas chafing, their clock in our ears,
     time at a standstill—

then, Pirandello's saracen olives
tortured out of the stony ground,
stumped by drought and turned in time
to crippled twists, gaping barks,
     an agony unwound,

and the hills infernally veined with sulphur,
fruit scented with the taste of hell,
that chthonic stench of a sapped underworld
and, in my piss, surprising, as if
     Persephone's self

passed in the stink of tinder and brimstone—
our old mineral complicity with earth,
filter of Hades, bitter mirth.
This acrid element will not leave,
     but seeps and stains

through vents and craters, faults and fumaroles.
Persephone's shuttle trails its taint
along the bloodstream, tricking the tongue
bittersweet, two-ways. Stone's a taste,
     the tale not done

but keeps a swing-door, way out, way in,
wished-for, shafting like a miners' lift-cage,
rooting darkly through a field of flowers.
And I, in some dead siding halted,
       remember that girl.

Luck-Penny

'Che futuro [What future's
ci può leggere il pozzo legible in a Doric
dorico, che memoria?' well, what memory?]

– Salvatore Quasimodo

The place was shut. So we wandered away
to the bone-yards, the pits, the sulphurous mud

where a silty drain left a mulch of waste,
and a tumble of rubbish dragged windwards, grounding

its bottles, cans, paper-bags, plastic cups,
the weather's round-ups, modernity's flak—

this earth accepting all the muck that comes
from bin and bunker, sewer and sphincter,

with a gift for hosting waifs and drifters,
bit-parts, off-cuts, dross and compost.

Then suddenly, beyond, we found them: the shrines,
primitive, ancient, low-walled circles,

the Cthonic Deities' earthbound cisterns
like calling pipes to the underworld,

where one lost daughter's return compelled
a seasonal story through the gates of hell.

For a wish, for luck, I dropped it in,
to hear how far, how long—to tap

those silent reaches, recce the fall.
No sound commuted, and the air was still.

An Almond at Halaesa

Another lost city's unearthed remains:
Halaesa—the language salts my tongue.

Uphill we climb above the lingual sea
where seven islands point the sound:

Ali, Fili, Sali . . . I sing,
a wishing rhyme to rope them in

to winds of Aeolus – a windbag trick
that sent old shiploads quickly back.

≲

I crack an almond with an ancient stone.
It rings one shot in the afternoon,

as shards of casing fallen apart
only make a sweetness taste more tart.

Punic, Minoan, Arabic, Norman,
the races came and left new names,

their antique dead in rooms of stone,
the casings cracked to show the bone;

while out there islands float, windblown . . .
What other boatloads, lost for home?

Necropolis at Kamarina

Seaward:

June has parched the teasels that line the shore,
scanning measures of an infinitely moving sea.
Each flowered, dessicated core's a punctual oval,

sac of seeds, spiked to tease the yarn
the ancients hung with loom-weights from below.
No one needs them now. They stalk our road.

The land is flat—*maquis*—but what are we,
wandering alive one day in the ways of the dead,
stepping lighter for all their ground's settlement?

The sea has nothing to say. It writes epic scenes
or scribbles a line at the foot of each blue page.
A dream of homing heaves within its cage.

Landward:

Limestone's a quilted cold on which things grow.
It sieves the rain through permeable sinks and caves,

accepts all weathers, chalks the coastal plain,
inhumes dawn-damp for reserve in the dog days.

The lightweight people have leeched their minerals, salts.
Whittled to spillikins, sketchy, they're roughly pressed

in foetal positions or, flat-out, laid to attention
as if some marvel held them openly amazed.

Onward:

Dear fellow-bones, homed in yet prepared to go,
each perishable cargo stored in its hard wrapping:

tomba a fossa, a lastra, enchytrismos,
baby-bones laid in clay storage jars, packed

in wine-stained amphorae—goods for sending, safe-keeping.
So what's the deal? Death's an export trading.

Light creatures, sticks, with little to show for cover;
limestone's a quilted cold—a first-last sleepover.

Pantalica

for Robert and Tertia, archaeologists

'o muove un canto in questa notte eterna.'
[or inspires a song in this eternal night.]
  – Salvatore Quasimodo, 'Insonnia: Necropoli di Pantalica'

The limestone's thousand eyeholes watch where we go.
Mostly, we see nothing in them unless, with luck,
  in the sudden torchlight's shock,
a bead, a shard, a tiny crumble of bones.
Deep in the cliff's apartments things come apart.

Four thousand rock-cut tombs weather the centuries.
We'll take the measure of them and draw to scale.
  This art leaves nothing over,
but marks each gaping cave where a bone might lie
loose in the grit—discard from the rat's larder.

Like *this*: long pin, with a twist of DNA,
a greeting flung, and met, three millennia later,
  tomb-raiders' throwaway.
Our shy touching, clear as the ping of an 'A',
finds a life long gone, once nerved and riddling.

Old thing! fellow-stuff—an X records where you lie.
Did you dream some night-long feast, a banquet set?
  or else, if tired, a sleep
safe in the rock's safe-keeping, sealed and stored?
Strange stories grow in the dark behind closed doors.

Here's fennel, capers, thyme, the cliff's footholds,
then fig, lentisk, pistachio in the lap of the valley.
  Beyond, the Anapo winds
twenty kilometres and more to the delta's outflow.
We live, work, breathe, in the rock's old shadow.

Sicilian Road

An open runway tacks and plays for time.
Its cursive outline coasts, then loops and veers
across the valley bottom, changing its mind,
turning aside from ease—there are heights to climb.

The hills above are black and secretive.
The road unravels a spoor, dangles a trail,
then takes the ground in its stride and picks, at last,
a path that starts to climb, barely at first,

rising on each stepped foot, aloof and clear
above this shaky land that cracks and gapes—
like something traced, freehand, above the facts,
a phrase spun out of air, and fixed in place.

Imagine a river on stilts, bird-flight on steps,
a flow expressed in the poised footwork of a dance,
a flourish made by a fool who bows to a king,
mocking the grandeur there, yet gracing him.

It runs far up into dark primitive hills—
from here, a skater's turn, a rope to the winds.
Imagine a wavelength braced, pinned on its way,
as if you dreamed a tune, and could make it stay.

Translations from
Leonardo Sciascia

La Sicilia, il suo cuore

'But Sicily is all a realm of fantasy and what can anyone do there without imagination?'

– Sciascia, *The Day of the Owl*

'Therefore, he translated not the words but the gesture . . .'

– Sciascia, *The Council of Egypt*

Note on the Translations

The Sicilian novelist Leonardo Sciascia was born in 1921 in Racalmuto, a small town in the sulphur-mining interior of south-western Sicily. 'The story of Sciascia has its roots in the sulphur fields', writes Claude Ambroise. The classical underworld of Vulcan and Persephone had, for Sciascia, its real-life equivalent in the stories of mining disasters recounted by his grandfather: stories of rockfalls, explosions, floods and dangerous acetylene gases. The yellow sulphur of this landscape once encouraged a goldrush fever that, for much of the nineteenth and early twentieth centuries, was unregulated and often catastrophic. In Sciascia's poetry the classical resonances of the landscape, its antiquity in story, are mingled with these more recent connotations of a fiery underworld.

In 1948, Leonardo's younger brother, Giuseppe, killed himself at the age of twenty-five. Leonardo, who provided the lines from Catullus for his brother's tombstone: 'With you was buried all our house, / with you perished all our joys— / joys which, in life, your sweet love nourished', fell into a state of prolonged melancholy. He never allowed himself to mention his brother's name again. But four years later, in 1952, he published a small volume of poems, *La Sicilia, il suo cuore* (*Sicily, its heart*), which discloses something of what he felt at the time. Except for one or two, these poems have not, to my knowledge, been translated into English, and remain largely unknown.

For each poem I offer two translations: the first a fairly strict rendering which conveys the sense and syntax, line by line, but loses, in the process, the rhythm of poetry; the second a free version which takes the original and gives a part interpretation, part variation on a theme. Between strict and free renderings, adherence to sense and adherence to the makings of a poem in English, I have tried to catch something of the original, even if only 'between'.

Translations from Leonardo Sciascia

Sicily, its Heart

Like Chagall, I'd like to gather up this land
into the target's motionless bull's-eye.
Not some slow carousel of images,
haloes of nostalgia—only
these curdled clouds,
crows flying slowly down;
and the burned stubble, the sparse trees
grained like filigree.
A myopic mirror of pain, a heavy destiny
of rains—so far off is summer
which here diffused its naked heat
in scales of light—and so unlike
this autumn, begun
without the voices of the grape harvest.
Silence gobbles everything up.
It cracks, if the pan-pipes
sound a strain, spreading profound panic.
The ancients did not laugh at this light,
choked by clouds, moaning
on stinted fields, bitter shores,
in the rheumy eye of the wellsprings;
nymphs, hotly chased,
did not hide from the gods here; trees
did not nourish fruit for heroes.
Here, Sicily listens for its own life.

Sicily, its Heart

Look sharp. Observe,
how else but in pain? this shortening mirror
where rains forget the sun-rays of summer,
        glamour turns ordinary,
and sourmilk clouds pack on the horizon,
                        a crow flies down,
down where this harvest never started.
Here, silence feasts on its own heart.

        But listen. Catch
the faintest stirrings of an antique flute,
panicky, profound. Tears well up,
        blurring the wellsprings.
Nymphs never played bo-peep among these trees,
                        fruitless and stark.
Gods gave no chase, heroes plucked no prize.
Here, Sicily listens for its own heart.

Translations from Leonardo Sciascia

In Memoriam

The long winter suddenly wears itself out
in March siroccos—a fable
of freezing sharpness that brings you, finally,
a death—just as these poppies
light up a fiery flowering of blood.
And the first roses lie close to your bloodless hands—
the first roses sprouted in this valley
of sulphur and olives, along dead sidings,
beside the muddy yellow waters
the Greeks called gold. And gold is what
we call your life—our own also,
whatever remains of it—while swallows
weave the evening with their flights—
this, my sad evening, which is also yours.

In Memoriam

Winter's fable brings a death in spring—
poppies flowered from Persephone's arms
are blood-red, blood-charged, remembering.

Roses seem rosy beside dead hands.
Sulphur's yellow gilds the mud-pools,
goldrush, our vice, gold, our lands.

Here's a forgotten siding, brother,
and an evening stitched by swallows' wings—
sad evening, mine, also yours, together.

Translations from Leonardo Sciascia

The Dead

The dead depart, inside a black hearse
encrusted with funerary gold, at the pace
of slow horses—and often,
for them, the band plays.
As they pass, women rush
to shut the windows of their homes,
shops are closed—there's barely a chink
through which to observe the family's grief,
the number of friends following behind,
the class of carriage, the number of wreaths.
Thus the dead depart, in my country;
windows and doors shut, as if to beg them
to pass quickly by, to forget
the women busy in their houses,
the shopkeeper who weighs and robs,
the little boy who plays and hates,
and all the living eyes which swarm
behind the pretence of closed shutters.

The Dead

Boxed, they depart.   Don't look, who?   peering through
chink or squinny   loop or outlook   hunch or squint

wishing not to   think or tangle   angling for it
that thing crossing   our too much boxed-in   busy living

keeping within   four square walls   each to our own
locksure peepholes   bolted windows   all our ways

of dreaming hating   playing cheating   keeping safe
for a while while   that thing passes   in time passing.

Translations from Leonardo Sciascia

Alive as Never Before

From the old cloister I enter the silence
of your avenues, between stone effigies
that flourish like ruins
in the greenest luxuriance of the grass;
and a rank odour of earth and leaves
encloses me in your stagnant autumn,
even though the sun
shines on the stones and memorials
or winter shivers in the cypresses.

Perpetual season of death—and I find myself
alive, loaded with words,
like that ham actor at the grave of Ophelia;
alive as never before, close to my dead.

Alive as Never Before

It strikes you, entering, from cloister to graveyard,
chiostro / inchiostro (like monk to ink,
vestige to verbiage, pain to prating,
from rotting earth to these earthed effigies)—

and I, histrionic, with a bellyful of words—
How long will a man lie i'th'earth
ere he rot? I quote, striking the match
of life on his death—a sulphurous light.

Translations from Leonardo Sciascia

To a Land Left Behind

It's restful to remember your overcast days,
your old houses which choke the streets,
the grand piazza full of black silent men.

Among these men I've learned grievous tales
of earth and sulphur, dark stories ripped
from the tragic white light of acetylene.

And the acetylene moon of your calm nights—
churches in the piazza in mourning shadows;
and the sulphur-workers' hollow step, as if their ways
traversed sepulchral caves, profound pits of death.

At dawn, the sky's a cold silver eardrum
vibrating long to the first voices; the cold houses;
everywhere the sadness of a trashed feast.

And sunsets through willows, the long whistle of trains;
the day wilting like a red geranium
in women looking out on the street's aerial prow.

A ship of melancholy opened for me its golden sails,
pity and love rediscovered ancient words.

To a Land Left Behind

Footsteps knocking on the underworld,
its brimstone mines and pits of disaster,
clip-clop in the early ear of the morning,
hollow steps, headed for the dark—

blindly, except for the acetylene light,
tunnel-vision to the stone's gold stuff
where, sulphur-fuming an air of death,
that ancient inferno welcomes them in.

And a ship of sadness with its golden sails
carries me back to my small-town tale,
in Greek, recalling *eleos kai eros*,
old words: the pity and love of things.

Translations from Leonardo Sciascia

Family Reunion

All stays unchanged in this room,
the clock stopped many years ago,
little blue-and-white statues on the shelves,
photographs wedged in the frames of mirrors,
ungainly lamps on the tables—and always
the copper stove, recalling for us
the return of cold days.
As if enclosed in a circle of boredom,
we abandon time's ruinous passing.
We might forget each and every word,
allow the silence to save us
and memory to fade bloodlessly
till a real fire comes to welcome us in.
But the dog confidently lifts up his nose,
a look brimming with ancient anguish;
and in the eyes of others I find myself
without any pity—in estranging pain
which dissolves human time in bitter syllables.

Family Reunion

We might forget the lot
in the unremembering silence of old time,
in the stopped clock of these family circles,
    we might not recall,

    till the loving dog comes nudging,
and the ancient memory of his anguished gaze
(Odysseus returned twenty years late)
    sees what I see:

    myself grown pitiless with pain,
estranged from home, its small-town boredom,
and turning life's hurt, the life that's mine,
    to syllables that bite.

Translations from Leonardo Sciascia

Hic et Nunc

I am a mutilated statue
at the bottom of clear waters.

Halted in a gesture—and broken.

Only a tremor of things
reflected—trees enskied
and quick flights—can give me
the thrill of time,
a way to change nothing into words.

Hic et Nunc

Stopped dead, I'm locked
in a broken gesture,

an ancient statue at the bottom of a lake.

Look, what I see's a world reflected,
sky trees, bird flights,
time changing my unchangingness,
and tiny tremors I cannot feel
turning the nothingness into words.

Translations from Leonardo Sciascia

Insomnia

The shrill laughter of Night
has opened in the silence
like a fatal vein.

And I've been hidden within myself,
a blind terrified prey,
without memory or hope of light.

Now, in these houses' look of dawn,
the place is a vessel weighing anchor—
its sharply outlined rigging of masts
tangles, for me, in a sail of death.

Insomnia

Someone laughs in the night
then splits his veins.

Time to go
like these houses at dawn—

a ship rigged and branching
with death's full sail.

Translations from Leonardo Sciascia

Dancers on the Train

They wear long skirts, rainbow
scarves—overcome, they fling down,
stretching long legs on the seats.
They bemoan the cost of hotels,
the rushed departures, sleep
cut short at dawn.
Their names—Monica, Marisa—
have the sad shine of cheap pearls
that young girls buy at the fairground.
Poor, chattery swallows that migrate
from desert to desert—
swallows exhausted before their spring.

They close their eyes; a cold
veil of sleep retraces their features,
a childhood of pain surfaces—pale,
with barely a breath of life
on the vibrant iris of their scarves.

Dancers on the Train

Pearls, won from the pallor of their names.
Pain, set in a spectrum of rainbow.
The goddess treads on colours of thin air,
severs life's breath, throws open its window.

Translations from Leonardo Sciascia

A Veil of Waters

A veil of waters, tremulous for outlets,
obliterates the earth. The long winter
leaves olive trees watchful, the bramble bitter,
and the slender almond
fine-traced against a luminous sky.
Life's sap seeks out that dried-up rancour,
dissolves the knots of a frozen pain.
Musically, a remote sense of pity
lights up its figure—like a ray
of green and silver
that shuts me into the heart of a mirror.

A Veil of Waters

What's veiled is mirrored.
What's dried finds sap.
What's hurt knows pity.
What's seen is heard.
What's green is silver.
What's shut is a mirror.

Translations from Leonardo Sciascia

April

I'm a racketeer of things, camorrista
sitting in an April sun, which risks
turning me to resentments and deceits.
I watch a children's game warm up,
a gentle brawl enchanted
with light, seeking its own heart of music;
perhaps its own heart of pain.
The town nearby seems drowning
in green; beyond this game
full of voices, there's nothing but a place of silence.

April

Myself's extortionate, a racketeer of things.
Even the sun corrupts to bitterness—

till I see that child's-play, magical with light,
a heart-found music like a heart-found pain.

The silence of the place, stone-deaf, stone-hearted,
holds these voices like a chant, enchanted.

Translations from Leonardo Sciascia

From the Train, Arriving at B***

The house is shimmering white on the seashore;
the palm protrudes high into the blue,
a greenery patched with the yellow of lemons,
that cold shadow under a weave of branches.
Sounds scream against the daylight's crystal,
a bright red boat, full of voices, departs.
The girl who emerges onto the beach
has forgotten the whispered secrets of the night;
she waves airily to callers on the boat,
to the marine-blue day, the sun already high;
then bends, *vivace*, to slacken her quick sandals.

From the Train, Arriving at B★★★

The air's clear mirror is a crystal ear.
Sounds are screams.
This patchworked green casts its cold shadow.
A red boat leaves.

A girl's high wave might conduct the day.
Night's a secret.
She bends to stay and, *vivace*, slips
a strap of her sandal.

Translations from Leonardo Sciascia

September Rain

Cranes slowly delineate the sky,
more urgent, still, is the clamour of crows;
and the first roll of thunder is sudden
among the clouds' white reefs,
the wind, a scare in the trees.
Rain comes on like a thick mist
noisily raising flocks of sparrows.
Now it pelts down on the vines, the olives;
at the fury of the lightning
old peasants turn to prayer.

But here's a liquid blue eye
opening the closed face of the sky;
slowly it widens to discover
the squinty pupil of the sun.
A radiating light clarifies
the furrow of the plough, the jewelled hedges;
between ever sparser leaves
snowy clusters of pistachios sparkle.

September Rain

What have they written, those Vs of migrating cranes?
     What do the crows say?
Sparrows have scattered wide at the approach of rain.
     Whose prayer will intercede?

The sun-god opens his eye, glancing slantwise,
     sharpening the furrows, spangling the hedges,
and exposes, between leaves, a prize like snow:
     the harvest's pistachios.

Translations from Leonardo Sciascia

End of Summer

After the harvest, barefoot boys invade
the almond groves—sceptres of misery
their long wavering canes.
Their needle-sharp eyes
winkle through branches, to find
each missed naked almond.
I hear the tap-tap of canes,
light thuds on the turf—sounds
of summer dying, an autumn
of downpours and the poor.

End of Summer

And after the harvest, hardship's lords.

Barefoot, hungry, their sceptre-canes
blindly waving, tap-tap, tap-tap,
sounding a passage, feeling their way
to each missed almond's packed case.

Summer's leavings, an autumn of rains.

Translations from Leonardo Sciascia

Wintry

The day's a piece of cloudy spun-glass,
things fragile and weighty—perhaps at a shout
the trees will collapse with a shrieking sound,
the cold moon will crumble. But suddenly,
like a blade, the sun descends
into the open windy street,
and lights up again in the old shops.

To exist—to scratch at
boredom's sheet of lead,
to draw out of lead
its own illusory spirit of silver,
at a shot of light to sparkle
like those old things in the shops.

Wintry

Mirror mirror
your leadweight backing holds the world's spun-glass,
a shriek might shatter
moon or trees—a splintered outlook,
whip-crack shiver in a looking-glass.

Mirror mirror
there's spirit of silver in a sheet of lead,
dead dull, until
you scratch it—scratch its boredom, then see
old things sunlit from antiquity.

Translations from Leonardo Sciascia

Piazzetta for a First Act

The fountain has summoned the houses
to a light sleep—

        and the moon summons
to love of the fountain.

Piazzetta for a First Act

Act 1, small square:

fountain   houses   moon

  a trickle   slumber

  listen   soon over

moon   love   fountain.

Translations from Leonardo Sciascia

To a Friend

If in your eyes I search
for what makes you different from myself,
your look touches me with hatred, fleetingly.
In the depths of your eyes, like a dead man
in a well, some malice poisons
the miserable things that you forgetfully hide.
Just so, the dog frenetically buries
the bone he's stolen – and instantly forgets.

And this alone is what you live for:
that in a moment—while I'm distracted—
you might deposit on my plate of poverty
the loathsome mess of a dead fly.

To a Friend

I search your eyes, knowing what I'll find:
a well where a dead man rots in water.

Whatever you hide's buried like that bone
a starving dog stole, and instantly forgot.

Look—my plate's empty except for this:
this poison, your own; this dead fly mess.

Translations from Leonardo Sciascia

The Night

Night falls blindly on the houses.
In it, what remains of our life
is an appalling death-mask—our final face
in the final night of the world.

The Night

Night, a blindness—blind man's bluff--
and all we are is an appalling death-mask,
a last stare in the world's last night,
a face of nothing in that nothing's face.

Translations from Leonardo Sciascia

Notes

LIFE FROM SIXTEEN ANGLES

Valerio Magrelli, 'Musica, musica', from *Il Sangue Amaro* (Torino: Giulio Einaudi, 2014), p. 93.

Anita Lasker-Wallfisch, *Inherit the Truth: 1939-1945* (London: dlm, 1996), p. 79.

Mark Davis, *West Riding Pauper Lunatic Asylum Through Time* (Stroud: Amberley Publishing) p. 67.

Angela Leighton, 'Wilderness', from *The Messages* (Shoestring Press, 2012), p. 20; 'Spills', from *A Cold Spell* (Shoestring Press, 2000), p. 9.

POEMS

Playing for Chopin—The 'Rainbow' prelude, Op. 28, was composed at Valdemossa, Majorca. The title was George Sand's, who claimed the piece sounded like the rain that dripped off the roof in the monastery where they stayed. The museum there holds, among other exhibits, Chopin's original piano, a Pleyel.

An Almond at Halaesa—Halaesa is the name of the archaeological site of a Greek city on the north coast of Sicily. It overlooks the seven Aeolian Islands, among them Alicudi, Filicudi and Salina.

Necropolis at Kamarina—A Greek burial site on the southern coast of Sicily. The three kinds of tomb are trench tomb, slab-lined tomb and storage jar burial, this last often used for the burial of children.

Pantalica—a site in southeast Sicily containing more than four thousand rock-cut tombs dating from the thirteenth to the seventh centuries BC.

TRANSLATIONS FROM SCIASCIA

Leonardo Sciascia, *La Sicilia, il suo cuore* (Milano: Adelphi Edizione, 1952; 2010).

Quotations in the introduction are translated from Matteo Collura, *Il Maestro di Regalpetra: Vita di Leonardo Sciascia* (Milano, Tascabili degli Editori Associati, 1996; 2007), pp. 46, 37.

Acknowledgements

As these poems, stories and translations took shape, many people: friends, family, colleagues and editors, have offered their comments and advice. Thanks to all whose generous scrutiny helped me to hear, from the angle of another pair of ears, where revisions or excisions were needed.

And special thanks to Michael Schmidt, my editor, who was receptive at the start to the idea of this volume, and then steered it, with welcome critical acumen, to its completion. Thanks too to Luke Allan for more intelligent editing, and copy-editing.

Trinity College, Cambridge provided the one invaluable commodity, without which writing of any kind cannot happen: time. For that, I am immensely grateful.

Early versions of a number of these poems have been published in various journals: 'Below-Stairs' (as 'Under the Stairs') in *The New Yorker*; 'November Song', 'Footing', 'Crocus', 'Sluice', and 'The Slipper Chapel' in the *TLS*; 'Docklands', 'Nativity', 'Pantalica', 'By the Fire', 'Sicilian Road' and 'A Little Poem for a Space' in *PN Review*; 'Bog Asphodel' and 'Sea Ears' in *Archipelago*; 'Pomegranate', 'Prelude for Chopin' and 'Lines at Break of Day' in *Notre Dame Review*; 'Easterly' in *The Dark Horse*. In addition, 'Dump' appeared in *The Arts of Peace*, ed. Adrian Blamires & Peter Robinson (Two Rivers Press, 2014), and 'Canticles for a Passion' on the *Tower Poetry* website, November 2015.

For permission to quote Valerio Magrelli's 'Musica, musica', grateful thanks to the author himself. For permission to publish translations of poems by Leonardo Sciascia, grateful thanks to the Leonardo Sciascia Estate (for copyright information, see p. 2).